quando eis ostendit dies quo
modo incipies uultus
eorum fulgere sicut sol.
& quomodo incipient
stellae assimilari lumini
quomodo nare rupti,
sciamus ecce do. quaestioni
bus, supradictis maiores
enim exultabunt cum fi
ducia. & qui confidesbunt
non confusi. & gau
debunt non reuertentes,
festinant cum uultum
conseruunt inuidores
& a quo incipiunt gloria
si mox eodem praeciperet,
in corde anima ruinius
cetera itaquo do inuita
ratur pdietatis eru
cetera qui sperauit a
modo quinque loceruit,
& respondi & dixi,
ergo dabit tempus ani
mabus postquam sepa
rati fuerint decoribus,
utueleant dequorum
dixerit, & dixit, sep
tem diebus erit libertas
earum utueleant quae
pdicta sermone.

et postea congregabuntur
in habitaculis suis, & respon
di & dixi, si inueniam
ante oculos suos demonstra
mihi adhuc seruo qui sim
diiudicii iustimpios & cui
qare poteritis; deprecatis
eis altissimum, si patres
p filiis uel filii pparentibus, si
fratres p fratribus, siuel
sui p proximis, si fideles
tes pro carissimis, uel qui
do carissimi, ut se
intelligat aut dormiat
aut manduces & aut curet, si sic
sicut ita nemo pro aliquo
agitur, Omnis cum patie
buntur unusquis que unicam
iustitias suas, aut iniustitias,
& respondi & dixi, & quo
modo inuenimus modo quim
roga p me abueham ppt
sdomitas, & moyses
p patribus, quim deserto
p peccauerunt, & iesus post
eum p prir, In diebus, a
chaz & samuel & dauid
p confractione, & solomon
peis quim sci fiernones
& helias phis quipluuiam

THE MISSING FRAGMENT

OF THE

LATIN TRANSLATION

OF

THE FOURTH BOOK OF EZRA,

DISCOVERED,

AND EDITED WITH AN INTRODUCTION AND NOTES,

BY

ROBERT L. BENSLY, M.A.

SUB-LIBRARIAN OF THE UNIVERSITY LIBRARY, AND READER IN HEBREW,
GONVILLE AND CAIUS COLLEGE, CAMBRIDGE.

EDITED FOR THE SYNDICS OF THE UNIVERSITY PRESS.

Cambridge:

AT THE UNIVERSITY PRESS.

London: CAMBRIDGE WAREHOUSE, 17, PATERNOSTER ROW.
Cambridge: DEIGHTON, BELL, AND CO.

1875.

CAMBRIDGE UNIVERSITY PRESS
Cambridge, New York, Melbourne, Madrid, Cape Town,
Singapore, São Paulo, Delhi, Mexico City

Cambridge University Press
The Edinburgh Building, Cambridge CB2 8RU, UK

Published in the United States of America by Cambridge University Press, New York

www.cambridge.org
Information on this title: www.cambridge.org/9781107620957

First published 1875
First paperback edition 2013

A catalogue record for this publication is available from the British Library

ISBN 978-1-107-62095-7 Paperback

TO MY FELLOW-WORKERS

IN THE

REVISION OF THE AUTHORIZED TRANSLATION

OF THE

HOLY BIBLE AND APOCRYPHA,

THESE PAGES ARE RESPECTFULLY DEDICATED.

INTRODUCTION.

IN the fourth book of Ezra (the second of Esdras in our Apocrypha) the transition from the thirty-fifth to the thirty-sixth verse of the seventh chapter must strike even a superficial reader as singularly abrupt[1]. That this want of coherence was felt by the earliest of modern commentators on the book, is proved by his elaborate attempt to supply a train of thought in order to bring the two verses into connexion[2]. It was not however till the beginning of the eighteenth century that appeal was made to another representative of the lost original. Then appeared Ockley's translation of the Arabic version[3], where between the verses in question a long passage intervenes,

---

[1] vii. **33.** "Et revelabitur Altissimus super sedem judicii, et pertransibunt miseriae, et longanimitas congregabitur.

34. Judicium autem solum remanebit, veritas stabit, et fides convalescet,

35. Et opus subsequetur, et merces ostendetur, et justitiae vigilabunt, et injustitiae non dominabuntur.

36. Et dixi: Primus Abraham propter Sodomitas oravit, et Moyses pro patribus qui in deserto peccaverunt,

37. Et qui post eum pro Israel"...Vulg. ed. Sabat.

[2] "Audiens Esdras judicium futurum, primum, et novissimum, de populo suo, maxime autem de abjectione synagogae Iudaicae, pro qua plurimum zelabat, quia in ejus locum surroganda esset sponsa ecclesia sine ruga, solicite inquirit ab angelo, si non sit relictus aliquis locus intercedendi pro eo populo, et clementiam impetrandi a pientissimo patre coelesti, cujus sunt infinitae miserationes. Si quo modo gratia implorari possit pro Israele, juxta carnem, ne omnino abjiciatur." Conr. Pellicanus, *Com. Bibl.* Tom. v. fol. Tiguri, 1538, p. 258.

B.

[3] Published in the Appendix to Vol. IV. of Whiston's *Primitive Christianity Reviv'd.* 8vo. London, 1711. The existence of this Arabic version had been pointed out by John Gregory, who in his zeal for Oriental learning overestimated its value: "I have cause to beleive, that it is the most authenticke remaine of this Booke." *Notes and Observations upon some Passages of Scripture.* 4to. Oxford, 1646, p. 77. The Arabic text itself, however, was not printed till 1863, by Ewald, in Vol. XI. of the *Abhandlungen der k. Gesellsch. der Wissenschaften zu Göttingen.* Ockley's English translation has been rendered into Latin by Hilgenfeld, with H. Steiner's corrections, in the *Messias Judæorum.* Lips. 1869. Hitherto only one MS. of this version has been used, viz. Bodl. 251, which has lost two leaves (containing iv. 24—45 and viii. 50—ix. 1). Ewald (*Das 4ᵗᵉ Ezrabuch*, p. 100) hints at the existence of another MS. in the Vatican, and from Assemani's description, abridged by Mai (*Script. Vet. Nova Coll.* Vol. IV.), we may readily identify it with Cod. III. Assemani indeed denies the identity of 1 Ezra in this MS. with our 4 Ezra, but the order in which it

1

which carries on the thread of the narrative in an artless and appropriate manner[1]. In the present century the text of the Arabic has been printed, the long neglected Armenian translated[2], and the apparatus criticus of the book greatly increased by the publication of the text and translation of the following versions: the Aethiopic[3], the shorter Arabic[4] (Arab.[2]), and, last but not least, the Syriac[5], and in all of them the hiatus

stands, the title and the beginning which he quotes, are all the same as in the Bodl. MS., so that we may regard his language as a hasty conclusion based on the absence of chapters i. ii. xv. xvi. from the Arabic version.

[1] Yet the genuineness of this portion was not immediately recognized. Dr. Fr. Lee wrote thus to Ockley: "The *Arabic* Copy, or Version, besides many lesser Interpolations, hath a very large one concerning the intermediate State of Souls" (*An Epistolary Discourse concerning the Books of Ezra.* Lond. 1722, p. 21). P. J. S. Vogel held all between vii. 25 and *assumeretur* viii. 20, to be a later addition to the original (*Commentatio de Conjecturae usu in Crisi Novi Test., cui adjecta est altera de Quarto Libro Esdrae.* 4to. Altorfii, 1795), but the force of his arguments was considerably weakened by a few remarks of Laurence. Hilgenfeld still maintains the theory of an interpolation, but within narrower limits, viz. vii. 45—*Vicerit* vii. 115 (45).

[2] By J. H. Petermann, for Hilgenfeld's *Messias Jud.* The Armenian version itself was published as early as A.D. 1666, in the first edition of the Arm. Bible, according to Masch in Le Long's *Bibl. S.* II. 1, A.D. 1781, p. 175. Its existence therefore could scarcely have been unknown to scholars, as it is mentioned also by Bredenkamp (Eichhorn's *Allg. Bibl.* IV. A.D. 1792, p. 626), by Michel Tchamitchian (*Histoire d'Arménie.* 4to. Ven. 1784—86, Vol. III. p. 660; his statement, referred to by Scholz, that Usgan, the editor of the first Arm. Bible, translated 4 Ezra from the Lat. is obviously incorrect), by C. F. Neumann (*Versuch einer Gesch. der Armen. Lit.* A.D. 1836, p. 39), and by Scholz (*Einleitung* I. A.D. 1845, p. 501). But strange to say, this version appears to have escaped the notice of the editors of our book till pointed out by Ceriani, A.D. 1861 (see *Mon. Sacra et Prof.* v. fasc. 1, pp. 41—44).

[3] This version, which had been quoted occasionally by Ludolf, in his *Lex.* (see Van der Vlis, *Disp.*

Crit. de Ezrae Libr. Apocr. vulgo quarto dicto, p. 75), was published together with a Lat. and Engl. transl. by Laurence (*Primi Ezrae Libri, qui apud Vulg. appellatur quartus, Vers. Aeth.* Oxon. 1820), from a MS., which is now in the Bodl. Libr. (No. VII. Dillm. Cat.). Many conjectural emendations were proposed by Van der Vlis in the treatise just mentioned; and Dillmann has given from MSS. examined by him an important list of various readings, but without specifying his authorities (*Das vierte Ezrabuch......von Ewald,* pp. 92—100); finally Fr. Praetorius has, by the aid of Dillmann's variants and four additional MSS., revised the Lat. transl. of Laurence for Hilgenfeld's *Messias Jud.* The materials for a critical edition of the text, which is still a desideratum, have been increased lately by the addition to the Brit. Mus. of the Magdala collection of Aeth. MSS., which contains no less than eight copies of this book (see Prof. Wright's list in the *Zeitschr. der deutschen morgenl. Gesellsch.* XXIV. 1870, p. 590).

[4] Also published by Ewald in 1863 (*Abh. der k. Gesellsch. der Wissensch. zu Gött.* Vol. XI.), from MS. Hunt. 260 (*Bibl. Bodl. Codd. MSS. Orient. Cat.* II. ed. Nicoll, p. 11), and described by him in *Nachrichten von der Georg.-Aug. Univ. u. der k. Gesellsch. der Wissensch. zu Göttingen,* 1863; it has been translated into German by Steiner, in Hilgenf. *Zeitschrift,* Vol. XI. 1868. As Dr. Guidi has supplemented for me the imperfect notice printed by Mai on Cod. Ar. Vat. CCCCLXII. (*Script. V. N. coll.* IV.), I am able to announce the discovery of a second MS. of this version.

[5] A Latin translation of this version was printed by Dr. Ant. Ceriani in 1866 (*Monum. Sacra et Prof.* Vol. I. fasc. 2), and followed after a short interval by the publication of the Syriac text itself (*id.* Vol. v. fasc. 1, 1868) from the celebrated MS. of the Peshito (B. 21. Inf.) in the Ambrosian Library. The same scholar now proposes to reproduce by photolitho-

is found to be filled up in essentially the same way. As these versions seem generally to be of independent origin, and some are of considerable antiquity, their agreement

graphy the entire MS., which has been assigned to the sixth century.

There had long before been rumours of the existence of a Syriac version in a MS. once the property of Julius Caesar Scaliger, which Fabricius in vain attempted to discover (*Cod. Pseudepigr. Vet. Test.* ed. II. Vol. II. p. 176). The MS. in question is thus referred to by Scaliger himself: " Arcana vero multo plura continentur in libris Esdrae, atque potiora, quam quivis enarratione. Eos libros, quod hoc eloqui ausus es, suspicor te non vidisse: quorum admirabile, ao divinum compendium apud me est, Syra conscriptum lingua. In iis igitur longe, uti dicebam, praestantiores sententiae continentur, quam in concionibus sordidissimi calumniatoris, atque impurissimi impostoris Emanuelis." *Exotericarum Exercitationum Liber quintus decimus, de subtilitate ad Hieron. Cardanum.* 4to. Lutetiae, 1557, f. 422. Exerc. CCCVIII. ' an lectis audita jucundiora.' This can scarcely be an allusion to the 3rd and 4th books of Ezra, but rather, as Fabricius suggests, to what was supposed to be a Syriac compendium of the seventy secret books mentioned in 4 Ezra xiv. 46, 47. I believe that the very MS., which Scaliger could so safely flourish in the face of his opponent, is now in the University Library, Cambridge, marked MM. 6. 29. It treats of astrology and alchemy, and resembles, to some extent, MS. Egerton, 709, in the Brit. Mus. (described in the *Catal. of Syr. MSS.* by Prof. Wright, Vol. III. p. 1190).

From fol. 116 b. to fol. 120 a. of the Cambridge MS., we have what professes to be an extract from the Book of Ezra, the wise scribe,

ܪܐܙܐ ܪܐܝܢܐܝ ܪܟܬܒܐ ܡܢ ܥܘܕ ܡܪܢܐܝܢ

It commences thus:

ܡܢ ܐܬܘܬܐ ܕܐܝܬ݂ܝܐ ܝܐܪܝܐ ܡܪܐ ܡܢ ܐܘܪܫܝܡ ܩܘܢ ܣܒܘܡܐ ܡܢ ܗܘ ܪܝܒܐ

ܐܘ ܝ ܢ ܠ

This MS. once belonged to Erpenius, and came

into possession of the University together with his other MSS. in 1632. In the earliest printed catalogue of this collection it seems to be described as Liber theologicus mutilus, in 4. (*Petri Scriverii Manes Erpeniani.* 4to. Lugd. Bat. 1625). Erpenius probably received it from the younger Scaliger, and it is not unlikely that it was one of the libri Chaldaici in the possession of Jo. Picus Mirandula; that scholar, as we know, regarded the seventy books, above referred to, as a storehouse of mystic theosophy and cabbalistic lore, and I know of no other Syr. MS. that could in any degree justify, from his point of view, such glowing language as this: " Animarunt autem me, atque adeo agentem alia, vi compulerunt ad Arabum literas Chaldaeorumque perdiscendas, libri quidam utriusque linguae, qui profecto non temere, aut fortuito, sed Dei consilio, et meis studiis bene faventis Numinis, ad meas manus pervenerunt. Audi inscriptiones, vadimonium deseres: Chaldaici hi libri sunt, si libri sunt, et non thesauri. In patris Ezre, Zoroastris, et Melchiar Magorum oracula, in quibus et illa quoque, quae apud Graecos mendosa et mutila circumferuntur, leguntur integra, et absoluta: tum est in illa Chaldaeorum sapientum, brevis quidem et salebrosa, sed plena mysteriis interpretatio. Est itidem et libellus de dogmatis Chaldaicae theologiae, tum Persarum, Graecorum, et Chaldaeorum in illa divina et locupletissima enarratione. Vide, Marsili, quae insperata mihi bona irrepserunt in sinum"... (*Opera Omnia,* fol. Bas. 1601, Vol. I. p. 249).

The report with regard to a Hebrew copy of this book rests only on a vague statement of an untrustworthy writer: *Tertium et quartum Ezrae Hebraicos adhuc ipse non vidi: quidam tamen ex ipsis aiunt, eos nuper inventos Constantinopoli reperiri.* Galatinus, *Opus de Arcanis Cathol. veritatis.* 1561, p. 2. Dr. Fr. Lee was entirely mistaken in supposing that the Hebrew words printed on the margin of this book in the Lat. Bible of H. Stephens 8vo. Lutet. [1545] were derived from a Hebrew copy, and even Laurence failed to remove all misapprehension on this point (*Primi Ezrae libr. vers. Aeth.* p. 301). The fact is that Petrus Cholinus (not Leo

on this point raises a strong presumption that the additional matter formed part of the Greek text from which they were derived. Not only so, but there is decisive evidence that the Latin version also once contained the passage which is now absent; for Ambrose, in his treatise *De Bono Mortis*, drew largely for illustration from this version, and especially from the missing portion. The Benedictine editors of his works were perplexed at references which they could not verify, and suggested that a solution might be found in the examination of fresh MSS.[1] They casually refer to two, one of which belonged to their own library (at St. Germain des Prés); this was in all probability the 'MS. Sangermanensis' (Cod. S.), which a distinguished member of this order (Pet. Sabatier) upwards of sixty years later made use of for his great work, especially in the fourth book of Ezra. In late years it has been collated in a few passages by Dr. Hase for Volckmar's *Esdra Propheta*, and very fully by Dr. Zotenberg for Hilgen-

---

Judaeus), who modernized the Latin version of this book, occasionally added on the margin, not only in this, but in the other apocryphal books, a Hebrew equivalent where it seemed to throw a light on the peculiar use of a Latin word or phrase. E. g. chap. iv. 52, *De signis de quibus me interrogas*, stands thus in the revised text: *Praesagitiones eorum de quibus me interrogas*, with the marginal note מפתים *indicia*, vaticinia seu praedictiones. v. 42, *novissimorum tarditas;* in the revised text: *posteriorum tarditas*, with the marg. note אחרונים; similarly in other places. vii. 33, *et longanimitas congregabitur;* in the revised text: *et finis imponetur patientiae*, marg. יאסף. In the same way a Greek word is sometimes introduced, and yet no one has ventured to maintain that the Greek was still extant. As in chap. x. 14, *ab initio ei qui fecit eam* [=terram]; in the revised text: *homini qui eam jam inde ab initio exercuit*, marg. ἐργάζεσθαι, facere et colere, ut et עבד. xiv. 9, *converteris;* in the revised text: *conversaberis*, marg. ἀναστρέψῃ.

[1] "Quin etiam eumdem hunc librum inter canonicos descriptum in quibusdam antiqui ævi MSS. reperire est, non tamen in omnibus, nec sine discrimine aliquo. Namque in quodam pervetusto codice qui nostra in Bibliotheca adservatur, compactis in unum duobus canonicis libris Esdræ, secundus a primo capite hujusce quarti sumit exordium, haud dubie quia ejus illud initium est: *Liber Esdrae Prophetae secundus:* tum ex ejus atque tertii libri capitibus inter se permixtis quatuor libelli conficiuntur. Doctissimus Faber Ludovici XIII. præceptor quemdam ejusdem quarti libri MS. adeo discrepare ab editione deprehendit, ut varias ejus lectiones Card. Baronio transmittendas putaret. Quae diversitas forte in causa est, cur nonnulla ab Ambrosio ex eodem libro citata in edito minime reperiantur." S. Ambrosii *Opp.* fol. Par. 1686, Vol. I. 388.

The following is the passage referred to from the letter of Nic. Faber to Card. Baronius:

"Porro his litteris adiunxi exemplar donationis Othonis tertij discipuli Gerberti qui Siluester 2. dictus est, ex eodem illo volumine instrumentorum cuius supra mentionem feci transcriptum: tum etiam duorum capitum priorum libri quarti Esdræ ex manuscripto Bibliorum codice non admodum vetusto ab editis valde dissidentium, vtrumque, ni fallor, valde sublestæ fidei...

...... Duo autem illa capita, quod eam varietatem libri licet apocryphi antiquissimi tamen, cuiusque magni viri Clemens Alexandrinus & B. Ambrosius auctoritatem non defugerunt, doctissimis illis viris qui elegantissimis vtriusque linguae Bibliorum editionibus præfuerunt non ingratam fore existimauerim, & in eo vtilem quod ex isto fragmento quædam in editis emendanda percepturi sint." Nic. Fabri *Opuscula*, Par. 1618, p. 107.

feld's *Messias Judæorum,* and it is now regarded by the common consent of scholars as the oldest and best authority for the Latin text of our book. It is in the second volume of the Latin Bible now numbered MS. 11504, 11505, fonds Latin, Bibl. Nat., Paris[1]. Sabatier described it as nine hundred years old at the time when he wrote (1751), and editors invariably speak of it in general terms as a MS. of the ninth century, but the precise date at which it was written is recorded in the MS. itself, viz. the eighth year of Louis le Débonnaire (= A.D. 822). Great as is the critical value of this MS., a still higher interest attaches to it in the history of the transmission of our book of Ezra, for the researches of Prof. Gildemeister lead to the conclusion that it once contained the lost verses, and that it is the parent of all later MSS. The following extract, translated from a letter which he has kindly sent me on the subject, will explain the process by which he has arrived at this important result:

"On collating the Codex Sangermanensis in 1865, I discovered that the missing passage between chap. vii. 35 and 36 was once contained therein. The verso of one leaf ends with: *et iniustitiae non dormibunt,* and the recto of the next begins with: *primus* (with a small *p*) *Abraham propter Sodomitas et Moyses.* But a leaf which originally came between (it was the sixth of the quire, if I am not mistaken) has been cut out, leaving about half an inch of its inner margin, so that the corresponding leaf remains fast in the binding. The inevitable inference then is that all known MSS., since none have been found without this lacuna, were derived from the Codex Sangermanensis. And this I have found fully confirmed by arguments drawn from the state of the text in the MSS. themselves; for I have myself collated a considerable number in the course of many years, and have been able to trace the gradual and at the same time arbitrary changes continually going on till the appearance of the first printed edition."

These remarks set vividly before us the high importance which would attach to the discovery of a MS. of this book, at least as old as the Cod. Sangerm. The existence of such a MS. in one of the libraries of Europe could scarcely be looked on as beyond the bounds of possibility, especially when we consider how large a field remained unexplored owing to the imperfect notices of the contents of a Lat. Bible given even in some of the better Catalogues of MSS. I have therefore for several

[1] See the reff. in *Nouveau Traité de Diplomatique,* Vol. VI. p. 638, and especially the Comte de Bastard's costly work, *Peintures des MSS. depuis le huitième siècle jusqu'à la fin du seizième,* dix-septième Livraison (1842), which contains a facsimile of 4 Ezra xvi. 78.

years availed myself of every opportunity of examining Latin biblical MSS. The book itself is not, according to my experience, so uncommon as is generally supposed[1]; I found it in many Codices ranging from the thirteenth to the fifteenth centuries, but never without the lacuna. Meanwhile an article in the Catalogue of MSS. belonging to the Bibliothèque Communale of Amiens, by Mons. J. Garnier, 8vo. Amiens, 1843, had caught my eye—it runs thus:

"10. Libri Esdrae. Vélin in-4°. 83 f.

d. r. L.[2] Corbie. 174. A.

IXe. siècle. Ecriture minuscule rapide, peu soignée et de plusieurs mains, à 2 colonnes de 30 lignes, non réglées. Le premier feuillet est à demi détruit.

Esdras est ici divisé en 5 livres. Le 1er. est composé des deux livres d'Esdras, appelés Canoniques; les quatre autres comprennent le 3e. et le 4e. de la Vulgate.

Le 2e. du MS. est le 3e. de la Vulgate; le 3e. comprend les deux premiers chapitres; le 4e. les chapitres 3 à 15; le 5e. les chapitres 15 à 16 du 4e. livre.

On lit à la fin: *Finit liber quintus Esdre profaete deo gratias ago pro hoc facto perfecto*. On y lisait autrefois: *Finiunt quinque libri*, mais ces trois mots ont été effacés pour y substituer l'autre formule.

A la suite est la préface de St. Jérôme *Utrum difficilius*. C'est sans doute cette division d'Esdras qui a fait dire à l'auteur du Catalogue de Corbie, à l'article de ce MS.: *Cela paraît curieux à examiner*. A moins qu'il n'ait entendu par là, les mots *abhinc non recipitur* ajoutés en tête du 2e livre, et non *adhuc non recipitur*, comme on voit dans le catalogue publié par Montfaucon, qui désigne ainsi ce MS.: *Item*

---

[1] Laurence thus sums up the result of his investigations: " As the fourth book of Esdras was not translated by Jerome, it is of very rare occurrence in the MSS. of the Latin Bible. I have examined in all 187 MSS., 117 of which are in Oxford; viz. 86 in the Bodleian Library, 7 in St John's, 6 in Christ Church, 5 in Brazen Nose, 4 in New College, 4 in Magdalen, 3 in Corpus Christi, and 2 in the Radcliffe Library; the remaining 70 being in the British Museum; but I have found it in only 13; viz. in 3 at the Bodleian, in 2 at New College, in 1 at Magdalen, and in 7 at the British Museum" (*Primi Ezrae libri...versio Aeth.* p. 283). My researches among the libraries at Cambridge give a higher average. I have examined a little more than 100 MSS. of the Latin Bible, and have found it in 12; viz. in 2 at the University Library, in 2 at St. Peter's, in 2 at St. John's, in 1 at Gonville and Caius, in 1 at St. Catharine's, in 1 at Jesus, in 1 at Emmanuel, in 1 at Sidney Sussex, and in 1 at the Fitzwilliam Museum; besides this, chapters I. II., alone, are found in one MS. of the University Library and in one of Magdalene.

[2] i. e. Demi reliure de M. Le Prince, about whom M. Garnier has the following interesting notice: " M. Le Prince aîné, qui venait de quitter le commerce, offrit de consacrer ses loisirs à la reliure de ces volumes. Dès lors il alla à Paris étudier cet art auquel il était tout-à-fait étranger, et après un apprentissage qui dura près d'une année, il se créa

*2 libri primi Esdrae semel et iterum et duo postremi semel tantum. cod. memb. saec. 9.
nota quod initio 2 postremorum habetur eadem manu, Adhuc non recipitur."*

Amid the revived interest in apocryphal literature, which has sprung up in this
generation, and which has been especially concentrated on the criticism of the fourth
book of Ezra, it struck me as very strange that so early a MS. should remain uncol-
lated, nay, actually unnoticed, even by the three diligent scholars, Volckmar, Hilgenfeld, and Fritzsche, who have edited the Latin text in the course of the last twelve
years. I pointed out to several learned friends the necessity of examining this copy,
but, as nothing was done, I at last undertook the task myself. The perusal of a
few verses served to shew the great value of this new critical aid; I read on with
growing interest till I approached the place of the long-familiar chasm, then as my
eye glided on to the words *et apparebit locus tormenti*, I knew that the oldest and the
best translation of this passage was at last recovered, that another fragment of the
old Latin was gathered up, and that now at last—an event which can scarcely happen
again in these latter days—a new chapter would be added to the Apocrypha of our
Bible[1].

It will be seen that this MS. of the books of Ezra once belonged to the Benedictine Abbey of Corbie, in the neighbourhood of Amiens. The history of the library
of this abbey has been graphically told by M. L. Delisle[2]. It appears that it had for

un atelier, revint à Amiens et, avec un zèle et une
générosité sans exemple, donna à plus de 500 volumes
et à ses frais, une reliure simple, riche, solide et
convenable." (*Cat.* p. xxxi.)

[1] It would have been well if the compilers of our
Articles had avoided the appearance of claiming
even the qualified approval of Jerome for the 3rd
and 4th of Ezra. "And the other books (as Hie-
rome saith) the Church doth read for example of
life and instruction of manners, but yet doth it not
apply them to establish any doctrine. Such are
these following: the third book of Esdras, the fourth
book of Esdras, etc." Art. VI. The language of
Jerome here referred to is used by him expressly of
Judith, Tob., the books of Macc., Wisd. and Ecclus.
(*In Libros Salomonis, Chromatio et Heliodoro*, ed.
Ben. I. 938, 939). He speaks in other terms of these
books of Ezra: "Nec quemquam moveat quod unus
a nobis editus liber est: nec apocryphorum tertii et

quarti somniis delectetur: quia et apud Hebraeos
Esdrae Nehemiaeque sermones in unum volumen
coarctantur: et quae non habentur apud illos, nec
de vigintiquatuor senibus sunt, procul abjicienda"
(*Ad Domnionem et Rogatianum in Esdr. et Neh.
Praef.*). Again, of the 4 Ezra: "Et proponis mihi
librum apocryphum, qui sub nomine Esdrae a te et
similibus tui legitur...quem ego librum nunquam legi.
Quid enim necesse est in manus sumere, quod Ecclesia non recipit?" (*Adv. Vigilantium*, ed. Ben. IV. 283).

[2] *Bibliothèque de l'École des Chartes*, 1860, on
p. 438 he sums up the history thus: "La bibliothèque de Corbie, l'une des plus considérables qui
aient existé en France au moyen âge, est unique-
ment due au zèle des moines, qui, depuis le huitième
siècle jusqu'au quinzième, travaillèrent sans relâche
à l'enrichir, soit en copiant, soit en achetant des
MSS. Les trésors patiemment amassés pendant
près de huit cents ans sont dilapidés au seizième et

a long time been exposed to pillage, and when in 1636 Corbie was recaptured from the Spaniards by the troops of Louis XIII. it was thought advisable to transfer the most valuable portion of the literary treasures to the security of the capital of the kingdom. In consequence of a petition of the monks, four hundred select MSS., which had been taken to Paris, were not alienated from the order, but deposited in the Benedictine Abbey of St. Germain des Prés, *n'ayant personne qui soit si jaloux de conserver l'héritage de leurs pères que les propres enfants*. At the end of the next century these were transferred, somewhat diminished in number, to the Bibliothèque Nationale. The MSS. left at Corbie were removed to Amiens, probably in 1791, but from these again a selection was made, and seventy-five were sent to the Bibliothèque Nationale in 1803. The residuum however left at Amiens is by no means a contemptible collection, for it contains several MSS. of the ninth century, and among them the Lat. Version of the commentary of Theodore of Mopsuestia on the shorter epistles of St. Paul[1], which till lately was thought to be unique, and the volume which has furnished materials for the present work. Thus by a strange fatality the latter MS. has been lost in provincial obscurity, for had it been despatched to Paris with the four hundred in the seventeenth century, it would certainly have been examined by Sabatier; and if sent later, with the seventy-five, it could scarcely have escaped the notice of the scholars of the present century.

au commencement du dix-septième siècle. Beaucoup de MSS. de Corbie passent alors dans différentes collections particulières. Restaurée par les religieux de la congrégation de St. Maur, la bibliothèque de Corbie est menacée d'une suppression complète à la suite de la reprise de la ville de Corbie en 1636 par les troupes de Louis XIII. En 1638, quatre cents MSS., choisis parmi les plus importants, sont envoyés à Saint-Germain des Prés; de là ils arrivèrent à la Bibliothèque nationale en 1795 et 1796, à l'exception d'environ vingt-cinq volumes, qui avaient été volés en 1791, et qui doivent être pour la plupart à St. Pétersbourg. L'abbaye de Corbie conserva jusqu'à la Révolution près de quatre cents MSS. qu'on n'avait pas jugé à propos de porter à Paris en 1638. Cette suite de MSS., dans laquelle soixante-quinze volumes ont été pris en 1803 pour la Bibliothèque nationale, forme le fonds le plus curieux de la bibliothèque d'Amiens."

[1] No. 88, Corbie 51. F. It was published (the Com. on Gal., Eph., and Philem. entire, and various readings only of the rest, resulting from a collation with what Rabanus Maurus had introduced under the name of Ambrose, in his commentary on these Epistles) by J. B. Pitra (*Spic. Solesm.* I. 1852), but erroneously assigned by him to Hilary of Poitiers (so cited even by Rönsch, *Itala u. Vulg.* ed. 2, p. 526). The true authorship was first discovered by Prof. J. L. Jacobi (*Deutsche Zeitschrift für Christliche Wissenschaft u. Christliches Leben* 1854, pp. 245—253), who subsequently edited the Com. on Phil., Col., and 1, 2 Thess. in five University Programmes, Halle, 1855—66 (the 4th and 5th are both entitled 'Pars IV.'). Mr. Hort, who arrived independently at the conclusion that Theodore of Mopsuestia was the author (*Journal of Classical and Sacred Philology*, Vol. IV. pp. 302—308. Cambridge, 1859), has lately recognized the same work in an anonymous exposition of St. Paul's Epistles among the treasures of the Brit. Museum (MS. Harl. 3063); so that all seems fully ripe for a complete critical edition of this valuable commentary.

I now proceed to give a more detailed description of this Amiens MS. of our book, which I propose to call[1] Cod. A. It consists of 84 leaves of 11 × 7 inches (32,[2] v. and 84, r. and v. being blank), apportioned into 11 gatherings of 8 leaves each, except the 8th and 11th gathering, which have only 6 leaves apiece. The first ten gatherings have signatures by an early hand, from A to K; these signatures are on the last page, except B, which is on the first[3]. In the pages which immediately follow this Introduction, all that I have attempted, is to reproduce this portion of the MS., line for line as it now appears, so far as it can be exhibited by means of ordinary type. It is necessary to mention this, in order that it may not be mistaken for the original reading, which has been so tampered with by erasures[4], corrections, and additions, that it is often difficult to decipher. Further information on these points is given in the notes which follow (on pp. 51—54), where I have supplied, as far as I could, the letters which have been erased, and pointed out all that has been added by later hands. Being obliged to work at a distance from my MS., I have not been able to represent some characteristics of minor importance, such as the way in which words are spaced[5]. These and other defects may in some measure be remedied by the printed photograph of a page (fol. 65, r. chap. vii. 97—109 (39)), which I have inserted; but it is hoped that the Palæographical Society will undertake to perpetuate by indelible facsimiles the

---

[1] The letter A can scarcely be regarded as pre-occupied, since it has only been used by one editor (Fritzsche) to denote the Bibl. Eccles. Aniciensis Velaunorum, Tom. ii., e bibliotheca Colbertina (Cat. Codd. MSS. Biblioth. Reg. Pars iii. Tom. iii. Paris, 1744, page 1, No. IV.), which contains no more of our book than the 'Confessio Hesdrae' (chap. viii. 20—36) written in smaller characters at the end of Nehemiah.

[2] This blank comes in the middle of a verse; fol. 32, r. b ends with *uocate adolescentes* and fol. 33, r. a goes on with the next words: *et ipsi indicabunt*...3 Ezra iii. 16.

[3] As I have lately made use of a brief vacation to collate Cod. S., it may not be thought out of place to subjoin a few additional particulars with regard to that MS. The size of a leaf is 19½ × 13 inches; the gatherings are composed of 8 and occasionally of 10 leaves; the signatures, which in the Vol. examined by me are always on the last leaf, run on continuously from Vol. i. to Vol. ii. A slight

inspection sufficed to shew the correctness of Prof. Gildemeister's statement with regard to the excision of a leaf, for in the gathering marked xxxviii., where 4 Ezra is found, there are only 7 leaves, of these 1ʳ and 8 form a sheet, and so also 4 and 5; 2 and 7 are separate leaves pieced together, while 3 has no fellow, for 6 has been cut out with a knife, traces of which have been left on 5; the present pagination takes no account of this defect.

[4] I have inserted an asterisk to indicate an erasure (generally of a single letter), which has not been written over.

[5] The preposition and the word which follows generally cohere; chap. vi. 42 is a good illustration of the confusion which may arise from this habit of writing, here instead of *ut ex his sint*, Cod. A. has *ut exissent*, and for *a dō*, which stands both in Cod. A. and Cod. S., *adeo* is said to be the reading of Cod. T., and is adopted by Hilgenfeld and Fritzsche.

few precious pages, which have alone preserved this interesting fragment of the old Latin[1].

The character used in our MS. is the Carlovingian minuscule. Capitals are occasionally introduced at the beginning of paragraphs. Two forms of the first letter are used indiscriminately, viz. a and *a*, the latter sometimes resembles *cc* written closely together (see photograph, col. 1, l. 5). The diphthong is written *ae*, *œ* or *ǫ* (the lower loop in the last form is often added in different ink). The letters *b*, *d*, *h* and *l* are often thicker above and slightly curved. An instance of *c* joined by an upper stroke to *t* may be seen in the photograph, col. 2, line 28. A lengthened form of the letter *e* is frequently projected forward, especially on one of the letters *m*, *n*, *r*, *f*, *u* or *x*; a similar combination may be traced in the common form *&*, from which *ec*, as sometimes written, differs but slightly. The letter *i* coming after *l* or *t* is occasionally produced a little below the line, after *m* or *n* it is sometimes written entirely below the line (e. g. in fol. 62, v. b, line 26). The letter *n* sometimes takes the uncial shape, and is found so written, especially at the end of a line, in combination with a stilted *T* (see photograph, col. 1, l. 10), more frequently however the *t* in -*nt* has the appearance of a long sloping line notched above, springing from the last stroke of the ordinary *n* (see photograph, col. 1, l. 12). The stem of the *r* is often extended below the line, and sometimes this letter is so linked with a following *t*, that it might easily be mistaken for *f* (see photograph, col. 1, l. 28). The letter *r* generally takes another form when preceded by *o*, e. g. *o2*. The letter *y* is dotted thus: *ẏ*. I have given an approximation to the form of the stops as they now stand in the MS., but there are frequent traces of a corrector's hand in the signs of interpunctuation[2].

The following is a list of abbreviations which are found in Cod. A.[3]

---

[1] I notice on a second visit to Amiens, that the numbers of the chapters and also marks, shewing the beginning and end of this particular piece, have been lately added on the margin by the zealous librarian, who has taken a lively interest in my discovery.

[2] A not unusual mark of interpunctuation in Cod. S. consists of a comma with two dots, thus ⁖ as, for instance, *et delinquentes multos* ⁖ *Uidit anima mea* . . . chap. iii. 29. . . . *et abscondita est in infernum* ⁖ *fugit corruptio* . . . chap. viii. 53.

[3] In Cod. S. we have cū, ds̄, dn̄s̄, ē, ∴, &, ɪhs̄, ɪsrl, itaq: n̄r̄ɪ, q', q̄t (for *quod*), the usual compendia for *per*, *prae* and *pro*, sc̄a, sp̄m, s̄, superaueȓ, uastabunt², l intersected by a horizontal stroke for *uel*, ūrɪ̄: besides m̄s (= *meus*), om̄s with the last stroke of the m dropping below the line (= *omnis*), om̄s (= *omnes*); q̄ (= *quae*); secdm̄, sēcli, x̄p̄s̄; and among the corrections, f̄r̄ for *frater*. qm̄ is, if I am not mistaken, the uniform contraction for *quoniam* in Cod. S., and q̄m̄, not *quum*, is the reading of this MS. in vi. 8. The later sign for *et* (7) occurs in x. 5, but only as an insertion above the line. For *quisq*, see p. 29.

— over a vowel generally = *m*, as in *cū*, *cōmorantes*.

- b; = -*bus*, as in *temporib;*.

m̄ = *men*, as in *testam̄tis*.

-m⟋ = -*mus*, as in *altissim⟋*.

-r̄ = -*runt*, as in *fecēr*.

t' = *tur*, as in *t'batio*.

-t² = -*tur*, as in *ostendet²*.

t̄ = *ter*, as in *t̄minus*, *diligent̄*.

-ū = -*uit*, as in *plasmaū*.

-x̄ = -*xit*, as in *dedux̄*.

ʰ⫟ = *autem* (xiv. 24, 36).

d̄s̄ = *deus*.

d̄ō = *deo*.

d̄n̄s = *dominus*.

d̄n̄ı = *domini*.

d̄n̄e = *domine*.

ei' = *eius*.

ē =
÷ = ⎫ *est*.

prod÷ = *prodest*.

& = *et*.

dic& = *dicet*.

nequ&enebras = *neque tenebras*.

ı̄h̄s = *Iesus*.

ı̄s̄rl = *Israhel*.

mᶦ = *mihi*.

n̄ = *non*.

n̄r = *noster*.

p = *per*.

p̄ = *prae*.

p'm⟋ = *primus*.

℘ = *pro*.

q: =
q; = ⎫ *que*.

neq: =
neq; = ⎫ *neque*.

q' = *qui*.

q̄d = *quod*.

q̄m =
q̄n̄m = ⎫ *quoniam*.
quō =

s̄c̄m = *sanctum*.

scı̄ficationem = *sanctificationem*.

sp̄m̄ = *spiritum*.

s̄ = *sunt*.

tᶦ = *tibi*.

ū = *uel*.

ūri = *uestri*.

In the marginal and interlinear corrections are found other abbreviations, as: adūsus = *aduersus*, ꝗ = *que*, neqˑ = *neque*, sı̄c = *sicut*, and 1, with a horizontal stroke through the middle, for *uel*. The signs of abbreviation are sometimes altered or explained, generally by another hand, thus *ostendet'* is altered to *ostendet²* vii. 36, *finiant'* to *finiant²* xiv. 9, *porregebat'* to *porregebat²* xiv. 39, *siccabit'* to *siccabit²* xv. 50 (*scrutinatur* to *scrutinat²* xvi. 63). *uel* is substituted for ū ix. 34, ē for ÷ vii. 87, *terra* for *īra* vii. 62, ᵇⁱ is added over tⁱ vii. 44, ⁿ over ā in *quātū* vii. 74, and ⁱᵗ over ū in *plasmaū* vii. 94. Words to be transposed are marked thus ˇ*paradisus* ˇ*ostendetur* vii. 123 (53). Words to be inserted are indicated by ·/·, ⸲, : or · prefixed[1].

It may be here mentioned that there are a few omissions in the text of this MS., occasioned generally by homoeoteleuton, which have not been supplied at a later period, e.g. *et amici—inuenietur* v. 9, 10; *et incontinentia—iustitia* v. 10, 11; the greater portion of vii. 104, the three words at the end of viii. 39; *et altare—humiliatum est* x. 21, 22; *et de lingua—flammae* xiii. 10; the whole of xi. 27 and of xvi. 43.

Accents are by no means of rare occurrence; the following selection will give a fair idea of the way in which they are used[2]: *excídi* i. 20, *Iohélis* i. 39, *tuére* ii. 20, *consúmemus* iv. 15, *plasmátis* v. 26, *éa* vii. 74, *plásmatum* vii. 92, *adfínis* vii. 103, *ténebris* vii. 125 (55), *indignéris* viii. 30, *confidérunt* viii. 30, *amarísceris* viii. 34, *proximastí* viii. 47, *lugére* x. 4, 7, 9, 11, *próditi* x. 22, *páteris* x. 50, *conparére* xi. 19, *potióno* xiv. 38, *allídent* xv. 60, *odítā* xv. 60, *conbúret* xvi. 54.

uîs vi. 52, *mouéris* vii. 15, *loquéris* vii. 38, *fulgére* vii. 97, *coercére* vii. 116 (46), *solîus* vii. 118 (48).

The general characteristics of Cod. A. may be gathered from the following classified lists of its principal deviations from the textus receptus on points of orthography and grammar. As it will be convenient to have a comparative view of the distinctive features of the two leading MSS., I have attached an asterisk to every citation where Cod. A. and Cod. S. coincide, and have thrown into the foot-notes further examples of a similar kind from the latter MS. I have always quoted the original reading, and have not thought it necessary for my present purpose to record subsequent corrections.

The interchange of vowels:

a for **e**: *disparsisti* v. 28*, *insaniantes* xv. 30, *panna* xi. 12.

e for **a**: *castigere* v. 30, *praeparetum* ii. 13, *treiecientes* xii. 29 (*treicientes* Cod. S.).

a for **i**: *asaac* iii. 15, *chaemem* vii. 41.

---

[1] In Cod. S. words to be transposed are thus marked: ″*terram* ″*omnem* xv. 11; words to be inserted have ·/· prefixed.

[2] I subjoin a similar selection from Cod. S. *á* xvi. 16, 78, *áperi* v. 37, *éa* xvi. 8, *és* vi. 38, viii. 7, 37, etc. *hís* iv. 43, vi. 54, x. 59, xv. 45, xvi. 19, 21 etc. *hôs* xii. 24, *ó* iv. 38, vii. 118 (48), viii. 6. *tú* iv. 34.— Strokes over *i*: *ciliciís* xvi. 2, *initíum* xvi. 18.

conuertéris xiv. 9, *exîle* xii. 2, *pauêrem* x. 25, *persuadêre* x. 20, *radícis* iii. 22, *splendêrent* vi. 2.

i for **a**: *niscebar* v. 35.

a for **o**: *natho* xv. 39 (*natū* Cod. S.).

aa for **a**: *Ezraa* (voc.) xiv. 2, 38.

ae for **e**[1]: *adpraehendentur* v. 1, *aegimus* xii. 41, *Aegyptae* xvi. 1*, *aepuli* ix. 47, *aescas* ix. 34, *Aezra* vii. 2, *castae* vii. 122 (52), *conpraehendere* iv. 2, *depraecatio* xii. 7, *diae* vi. 53, *faciae* i. 11*, *faemur* xv. 36, *falsae* viii. 28, *famae* xv. 57, 58, *gaelus* vii. 41, *impiae* viii. 35, *intellegitae* vii. 37, *interpraetationes* xiv. 8, *inuanae* iv. 16, *ipsae* xiii. 26, *malae* vii. 121 (51), *praetiosa* vii. 57, *saecum* xi. 30, *saecundo* vi. 41, *saepulchrum* v. 35, *splendidae* viii. 29, *speciae* xv. 46, *uaenae* iv. 7, *uaer* vii. 41, *usquaequo* vi. 59.

e for **ae**: *Aezre* i. 1, *coherentes* xii. 19 (*quoherentes* Cod. S.), *meroribus* x. 12.

e for **i**[2]: *concedit* xiii. 11, *complecationem*[3] vii. 93, *demedii* xiii. 45, *eregere* xi. 25, *incederent* xiii. 23, *iteneris* xiii. 45, *perdedisti* iii. 9, *reieciet* v. 7, *sede* ix. 26, *sterelis* v. 1*, *uigelaui* xii. 3, and in the abl. *inimitabile* vi. 44.

i for **e**: *acciperunt* xiv. 30, *discendentem* xiii. 12, *interfici* i. 11*, *lugio* viii. 16, and in the old plur. termination *-is*, as *accipientis* viii. 56, *aduenientis* iv. 12, *dispositionis* iv. 23, *tristis* x. 8*, *uenientis* vii. 69.

-er for **-ur**[4]: *uiderenter* xiii. 11.

i for **ii**[5]: *labis* xiii. 10.

ii for **i**: *audii* vii. 2, *hii, hiis, lociis* xvi. 71, *nolii* ii. 27, *tenebriis* xiv. 20.

i inserted: *immaturios* vi. 21.

i for **u**: *corriptibile* vii. 96, *quadripedia* vii. 65.

i for **y**: *abisos* iii. 18, *Ægipto* xiv. 29, *Assiriorum* xiii. 40.

y for **i**: *cybabunt* xvi. 69, *Sydonis* i. 11, *sydus* xv. 13.

o for **u**[6]: *baiolans* iii. 21*, *edocauit* xvi. 68, *latibolis* ii. 31, *mormurastis* i. 15, *nas-*

---

[1] This change is not so common in Cod. S., it occurs however in a few other cases, besides those marked thus *: e.g. *aeducam* ii. 15, *aegenti* ii. 20, *aequi* xv. 35 (we have oe for e in *poenes* ii. 8). On the other hand examples of **e** for **ae** are much more numerous in this MS., e.g. *Abdie* i. 39, *acute* xvi. 13, *aduene* xvi. 41, *alique* xi. 21, *aque* iv. 49, *corone* v. 42, *deputate* vi. 57, *diuise, due* xi. 24, *leticia* i. 37, *mee* ii. 29, *passe* x. 22, *querentem* v. 34, *spice* iv. 32, with many others, especially the plurals of the 1st decl.

[2] In Cod. S. *abebo* xiv. 19, and some ablatives of the 3rd decl., as *de mare* xi. 1, xiii. 2, 5.

i for e: *exili* xii. 30, and in the pl. as *cogitationis* xvi. 55, *praesentis* v. 45, vi. 5, *similis* v. 52.

[3] Comp. Schuchardt, *Der Vocalismus des Vulgärlateins*, Vol. ii. p. 4.

[4] In Cod. S., *efficienter* viii. 50.

[5] In Cod. S., *ite fili* ii. 2; the converse, ii for i, does not seem to be so common in this MS.

[6] In Cod. S., *lapsos nostros* viii. 17, *tremor multos* xv. 36, *sobsessor* xv. 33.

u for o: *iustus omnes* iii. 11, *populus* acc. pl. iii. 12, *coadulescentia* iv. 10.

centor xii. 18, *tonicas* ii. 39*, and in the case-endings of substantives, so that the 2nd decl. becomes substituted for the 4th, *excesso* x. 37*, *flatos* v. 37*, *gemitos* i. 19*, *incenso* (sic) v. 1, *tumulto* xii. 2.

u for o: *agricula* viii. 41, *butro* ix. 21 (*butru* Cod. S.), *chaus* v. 8*, *cognuscere* ix. 12, *curuscabit* xvi. 10, *intrursus* xiv. 33, *nun* xvi. 10, *populus* (acc. pl.) i. 11*, *pupulum* vii. 129 (59), *prumptuariis* iv. 35*, *turmentis* xii. 26.

u for au[1]: *clusum* xiv. 41, *clusit* xvi. 59.

u inserted: *continguent* xiii. 32, *prolonguauit* xiv. 17.

The interchange of consonants:

b[2] for u: *praeteribit* vii. 46, etc.

u for b: *conlaudaueris* x. 16*, *conseruauis* xiv. 46, *multiplicauitur* v. 2*, *uiuificauit* v. 45*, etc., *odiuilem* xv. 48.

c for ch: *carta* xv. 2 (*cartha* Cod. S.).

ch for c: *Abbachuc* i. 40.

c for qu[3]: *cotidie* iv. 23*.

qu or q for c: *consequuti* ix. 10, *loqutus* xiii. 21.

c for t[4]: *iniciis* vii. 30*, *negociantur* xvi. 48, in vii. 98 *fiducia* has been altered to *fidutia*.

ch for h: *chaemem* vii. 41, *gechennae* vii. 36.

h for ch: *brahio* xv. 11.

ct for t: *conplecte* xi. 44 (*conplecta* Cod. A. sec. man. and Cod. S.).

d for t[5]: *quando* xii. 44; comp. *sedes* for *sitis* viii. 59.

t for d: *aliut* vi. 10*, etc., *aput* ix. 35, etc., *istut* i. 18, *situs* xv. 39.

f for ph: *Eufraten* xiii. 43, *Faraonem* i. 10, *Ferezeos* i. 21*, *Finees* i. 2*, *orfanum* ii. 20*, *profetiae* xv. 1, *Sofoniae* i. 40.

g for c: *gogitationibus* xv. 3.

h omitted[6]: *imnus* x. 22, *oras* ix. 44.

h prefixed: *habierunt* x. 22, *habundantiam* iii. 2*, [h]*arena* (sic) iv. 17 (*harene* Cod. S.),

---

[1] In Cod. S., *clusa* v. 37.

[2] In Cod. S., b for p: *obtabas* ii. 41, *obproprium* iv. 23.
ph for b: *Choreph* ii. 33.

[3] In Cod. S., *anticum* vii. 30 (*antiqum* Cod. A.).
qu for c: *quoherentes* xii. 19.

[4] In Cod. S., *iusticiae* vii. 35, *iniusticia* vi. 19,

iniusticiae vii. 35, *pudiciciam* vi. 32, *sicientes* i. 22.

[5] In Cod. S., *capud* xi. 31, *deliquid* viii. 35, *quodquod* ix. 10.
t for d: *quot* viii. 62, ix. 29, 34, x. 48.

[6] In Cod. S., *umidam* vi. 52.
h prefixed: *Danihelo* xii. 11, *helati* viii. 20.

Huriel v. 20 (*Hurihel* Cod. S.), *Johélis* i. 39*, *Israhel* iii. 32, etc., *Orihel* iv. 1 (*Horihel* Cod. S.).

n omitted: *contigebat* xi. 19, and in participles, as: *dices* vii. 38, *meties* ix. 1*.

n inserted[1]: *lingnum* i. 23, *millensima* vii. 138 (68)*, *praestans* viii. 8*, and so the *n* of the present is retained in the perfect and its derivatives, as: *derelinqui* x. 5, xii. 48*, *derelinquisti* xiii. 54, *derelinqueris* xii. 44* (comp. *delinquæt* viii. 35, *deliquid* Cod. S.), *uincerit* vii. 115 (45), 128 (58).

p inserted between **m** and **n**: *condempnare* iv. 18*.

t for **th**: *talamo* x. 1.

th for **t**: *notho* xv. 20.

ll for **l**: *camelli* xv. 36, *corruptella* vi. 28, vii. 113 (43), *medella* vii. 123* (53), *tutellam* i. 15.

mm for **m**: *mammellarum* viii. 10**[2].

nn for **n**: *Channaneos* i. 21.

rr for **r**: *corruscationem* vii. 40, *errant* xiii. 8, *conterretur* xvi. 11, *exterrent* xv. 43, 60, *exterrant* xv. 40, *exterruerunt* xv. 45*.

ss for **s**[3]: *Assia* xv. 46, *bellicossum* xiii. 9, *cassus* vii. 118 (48), etc. (but *casui* iii. 10*), *confussi* xvi. 66, *haessitemini* xvi. 76, *missit* xvi. 62, *possuit* xvi. 62, *possitum* xiv. 20, *repossita* xiii. 18, *quessiui* xiii. 7, *abussi* ix. 9, *uissionis* xii. 10, xiii. 25, *in uissionem* xiv. 17.

On the other hand:

f for **ff**: *dificile* vii. 59.

m for **mm**: *consumemus* iv. 15*.

s for **ss**: *abisos* iii. 18, *abv̇sos* viii. 23, *abv̇sum* xvi. 58, *carisimum* vii. 104, *confesi* ii. 47, *fisuris* xvi. 29, *fortasis* iv. 8, *misa* xvi. 16, *dimisa* xvi. 13, *emisa* xvi. 16, *inmisus* xvi. 3, *inmisa* xvi. 5, *inmisam* xvi. 7, *intermisione* x. 39, *promisum* vii. 119 (49), *presurae* ii. 27*, *abscisa* vii. 114 (44)*, *discisa* ix. 38*, *sesionem* ii. 23.

t for **tt**: *commitenda* i. 26*, *sagita* xvi. 16, *sagitam* xvi. 7, *sagitario* xvi. 7.

Non-assimilation[4]: *adcedebant*, *adfines*, *adligabit* xvi. 27, *adnuntia*, *adposui*, *adprehendere*, *adpropinquauit*, *adpropriauerunt*, *adsimilata*, *adsumeretur*, *adtendit*.

conlaudabunt, *conlident*, *conmirationem*, *conparuit*, *conponet*, *conpraehendere*.

---

[1] In Cod. S., *uidens* x. 42.

[2] There are not many examples in Cod. S. of this doubling of the consonant, yet there are two not found in Cod. A., viz. *Babillonem* iii. 28, *sum̄am* ii. 11.

[3] Cod. S. has **x** for **s**: *inextimabilis* viii. 21.

[4] In Cod. S. Non-assimilation: *adferet*, *adlident*, *adquesisti*, *adtamen*, *conburent*, *conprehendere*, *inmaturos*, *inreligiose*.

inlata*, inluminatus*, inmensum*, inmisit*, inmortale*, inpigri*, inproperauit*, inproperium*, inrita, inritauerunt, obprobrium (obproprium Cod. S.).

subpleam.

(**Assimilation**[1]: *accedat*, aspectus*, aspicias*, allident, apparuit*, appropinquat* viii. 61*, *collegi** etc., *irritum**.)

s retained after **ex**: *exspectate, exstiti, exsultatio, exsurget.*

s omitted after **ex**[2]: *exultant**.

Substantives: *opere*[3] for *opera* xiv. 21*, *nubs* xv. 34*, *uaso* vii. 88 (and in vi. 56, Cod. S.), *curris* for *curribus* xv. 29*[4], *sonus* for *soni* vi. 13*.

A neuter instead of a masc. termination, as: *conturbatum est intellectum tuum* x. 31*, *crescit sensum* vii. 64, *unde fructum fiat* viii. 6*, *factum est fructum* ix. 32*.

Adjectives and Pronouns[5]: *solo* (dat.) iii. 14*.

Sibimetipso xiii. 6 (comp. *sibimetipsos* Cod. S.), *tibimetipso* iv. 20*, and *haec* nom. pl. fem. vii. 80 (see note).

Verbs:

Under this head may be noticed: The frequent use of *-at* etc. for *-et* etc.[6], and vice versa, as: *deficiat* xv. 13, *ferant* vii. 18, *adferat* xiii. 23, *inducat* xv. 12, *rapiant* xvi. 47,—*colet* xvi. 25, *dispergentur* ii. 7, *faciem* i. 30, *reuertetur* xi. 46, *uiuent* xiv. 22.

The fut. of the 2nd conj. in *-eam*, as: *doceam* iv. 4*, x. 38* (but *docebis* xii. 38*), *respondeam* viii. 25* (comp. *appareas* xi. 45* Vulg.).

The fut. of the 3rd conj. in *-ebo*, as: *confidebunt* vii. 98 (see note).

The fut. of the 4th conj. in *-ibo*, as: *dormibunt* vii. 35* (comp. *custodiuit* for *-bit* xiii. 23* Vulg.).

The form *poterint*[7] for *-runt* vii. 102 (see note).

---

[1] (In Cod. S. Assimilation: *accedebant, annunciante* xi. 16, *irrita, irritauerunt, suppleam.*)

[2] In Cod. S., s omitted after **ex**: *expectate, extiti, exultatio.*

[3] There are more instances of this plur. in Cod. S., e.g. viii. 33 (where the word is omitted in A., but implied by the forms *multae repositae*), ix. 7, xiii. 23, xvi. 55.

[4] In Cod. S. we have the gen. *parti* (for *partus*) xvi. 39, *tumulti* xii. 2,—gen. pl. *mensum* vi. 21.

[5] *Illum* xvi. 40* is rather a masc. (the subst. *saeculum* taking its gend. from the Greek, see p. 18) than an archaic form for *illud.*

[6] In Cod. S., *bibant* xv. 58, *faciat* xv. 56. In this MS. *-bant* is often written for *-bunt*, as: *cogitabant* xiii. 31, *lugebant* xv. 44, *manducabant* xv. 58, *recapitulabant* xii. 25; and *-bunt* for *-bant*, as *habitabunt* iii. 12.

[7] Similarly in Cod. S., *erint* xvi. 66, 70, 72.

The following forms among the compounds of *-eo*: *exiebat* xi. 10*, xiii. 4*, *exientem* xii. 17*, *praeterientes* v. 55 (*praeterientis* Cod. S.), *prodientem* xvi. 39 (*prodiente* Cod. S.), *prodiendum* xvi. 40*.

The use of certain verbs as deponents[1], e. g. *certati sunt* vii. 92 (see note), *fluctuatur* xvi. 12*, *haessitemini* xvi. 76 (*esitemini* (sic) Cod. S.), *scrutinatur* xvi. 63, *trepidentur* xv. 29*.

The act. for the depon.[2], as: *consules* xii. 8 (*consulas* Cod. S.), *consolare* (inf.) x. 41*, *consulare* (inf.) x. 49, *demolient* xv. 42* (comp. the pass. in x. 21*, xv. 61*), *dominabit* iii. 28*, *dominare* (inf.) vi. 57, vii. 5, *dominauit* xi. 32 (*-bit* Cod. S.), *dominabunt* xii. 23*, *interpretaui* xii. 12*, *zelabo* xv. 52*, *zelabunt* ii. 28* (depon. in xvi. 49*, 50*, 51*).

Among compound verbs we find both *oboedierunt* i. 8, and *obaudire* i. 24*; both *adiecere* viii. 55, *proiece* i. 8, xiv. 14, *proiecientur* xvi. 24, *reieciet* v. 7, *treiecientes* xii. 29, and *adiciam* ix. 41*, *proiciam* i. 30*, 33*[3].

Adverbs:

certum xii. 7*, *inuanae* iv. 16, *iteratum* v. 13, *solum modum* vii. 54[4], *ualide* xiii. 8, in other places *ualde*.

Construction.

Prepositions joined to a wrong case[5]: *a sydus terribile* xv. 13 (*a sidus terr-* Cod. S.), *ad dextris* vii. 7, *coram quem* vii. 87 (see note), *ut essetis mihi in populo* i. 29, *eram in Babilonem* iii. 1*, *super tenebris nigrae* vii. 125 (55), *qui habitant in eum* xv. 14*.

Mistakes in gender[6]: *buxos multos* xiv. 24*, *finem suam* xii. 30*, *fontes meae* ii. 32, *labore multa* ix. 46, *sidus terribilem* xv. 40*, *somnii quem* xiii. 53*, *a multo timore quam* xii. 5*. There seems to be a tendency to use *factum est* (ἐγένετο) as a fixed form,

---

[1] In Cod. S., *somniatur* x. 36.

[2] In Cod. S., *scrutas* for *scrutaris* xii. 4.

[3] In Cod. S., *adicere, proice, proicientur, treicientes*.

[4] There are other instances in Cod. S., viz. viii. 5, ix. 24 (*solum modum flores*, but *solummodo de floribus* in the same verse) and xiii. 9.

[5] The scribe of Cod. S. indulges even more freely in this species of error; he confuses *a* (*ab*) and *ad*, as, *a te alia loquar* xiii. 56, *ab orientalem* xv. 39, *ad dextera parte* xi. 12, *ad dextra parte* xi. 20, 35, xii. 29, *ad leua* xi. 35 (comp. 'à droite,' 'à gauche'), *ad eminenti* xvi. 61, *uade ad me* v. 19, *recessit ad me*

v. 19, and deals thus with other prepositions: *cum laborem* x. 47, *de mare* xi. 1, xii. 11, xiii. 2, 5, *de omnem hominem* viii. 15, comp. viii. 16, 55, xi. 10, xvi. 73, *profectus est... in ciuitate* xii. 50, *post aliis tres dies* xiii. 56, *prae multos* x. 57, *pro desolationem* xii. 48. Cases like *ex* with the gen. v. 23, 24 (Codd. A., S.), and *de* with the gen. xi. 29 (Cod. S. and apparently in Cod. A. originally), are in imitation of the Greek.

[6] Add from Cod. S., *omnis corpus* xii. 3, *nubem, quem* xv. 39, *paradiso, quam plantauit*, iii. 6, *est factum... casus* vii. 118 (48).

B.

independent of the gender of the subject, as: *factum est permanens infirmitas* iii. 22 (comp. *et factum est species uultus eius altera* Luc. ix. 29 Cod. Amiat.) ; similarly, *et cum* (om. *cum* Cod. A.) *adhuc esset eis apertum poenitentiae locus* ix. 12*.

Sometimes the mistake in gender seems to be due to the influence of the Greek, as in the following examples: *creatus est saeculum* (ὁ αἰών) vi. 59, *qui nondum uigilat saeculum* vii. 31*, *saeculum qui ab eo factus est* ix. 2*, *certaminis* (ἀγῶνος) *quem* vii. 127 (57)*, *in campum* (τὸ πεδίον) *quod uocatur* ix. 26*, *omnem peccatum* (ἁμαρτίαν) xvi. 51*, *hoc enim erat duorum capitum* (κεφαλῶν) *maior* xi. 29*, *multitudinem* (τὸ πλῆθος) ...*quod paratum erat* xiii. 11*.

Among other peculiarities of construction may be noticed[1]: *obliuisci* with acc. of pers. i. 6* (with gen. i. 14*, xii. 47*); *obaudire* with acc. i. 24*; the double acc. with certain verbs, as: *folia arborum uos texi* i. 20* (comp. Ezech. xviii. 7 Hebr., and LXX. Alex., Luc. xxiii. 11, Cod. Bezae, Gk. and Lat.), *bibe quod te potiono* xiv. 38* (comp. Ps. lxix. 22 Hebr., LXX., Lat., Cod. Sangerm.)[2]; instances of twofold government, as: *nolite similari* (-*ure* Cod. A., pr. m.), *eam nec operibus eius* xvi. 52*; the inf. preceded by *ad*, as: *ad expugnare* xiii. 28*, 34, see Rönsch (*It. u. Vulg.* p. 430), who compares *à* before the inf. in French; a more general use of *et* to introduce an apodosis after *et factum est*, as in *et missus est* vii. 1*, *et feci* ix. 47*; the omission of the substantive verb in a relative clause, as: *his qui nunc* ix. 18*, *qui cum eo* xi. 31.

Very few of the anomalies exhibited in the foregoing examples have escaped revision. In both MSS. the hands of correctors, some of an early date, have been busy at work, assimilating the abnormal spelling, inflection, and construction to the classical standard of biblical Latin. Thus not only much that was rustic and rugged has been polished, but many an archaic form and phrase has been swept away, which constituted a marked feature of the original translation. Alterations meet us at every step: a letter regarded as superfluous has a short stroke or point (sometimes two points) below it (the points are often placed above in Cod. S.), or is erased. The most common corrections are *o* with *v* written above, *u* by a slight curve converted to *o*, *i* by a loop in lighter ink to *e*, and *e* to *i* by a long line drawn through it: *u* is changed by a continuation of its first stroke to *b*. The *et* of the apodosis was a frequent stumbling-block to the revisers, and there are many cases where it has been obscured or obliterated. The numerous corrections, and especially the erasures, form the chief difficulty

---

[1] Cod. S. has *parcentes* with acc. xvi. 72.   [2] For *arguo* with double acc., see below, p. 33.

in the collation of these MSS., and sometimes I have only been able to ascertain the genuine reading by a careful comparison of the faint traces left in the two MSS.

I have thus attempted to describe in detail the chief peculiarities of these two MSS., on account of the foremost rank which they will henceforth hold in settling the text of the Latin translation of the 4th book of Ezra. Nothing remains now but to consider the particular arguments in virtue of which Cod. S. is claimed as the ultimate source of all later MSS., and then to determine the relation in which Cod. A. stands to it, and the value to be assigned to this new authority in the criticism of the book. In pursuance of the first of these objects, I now resume my translation of Prof. Gildemeister's important letter at the point where he adduces various examples in proof of his statement that all later MSS. may be traced back to Cod. S. The foot-notes exhibit the readings of MSS. collated by myself.

In vi. 12, Cod. S. has *sequente praecedente*, the former word being dotted above as erroneous; in five[1] later MSS. both these words are found. In the same verse, Cod. S. and one MS. besides have *ex parte*[2], another has *parte*, which the rest have converted into *partem*. In iv. 23, *data est*, the original reading of Cod. S., has been corrected to *deducta est;* here one MS. gives *data est deducta*, the first word dotted below. In iv. 24, Cod. S. had originally *nostra et pauor*, but *et* is altered, probably by the first hand, to *est* (thus: *ēt*), and most MSS. have this reading; but one has *et pauor*[3], which was corrected in others to *ut pauor*, and in the printed text to *...nostra stupor et pauor*. In iii. 8, Cod. S. has the reading *in ira*[4], in which it is followed by a number of MSS.; in some this passes into *mira*, in others into *iniqua*. The number of these examples might be considerably increased."

"In the very inaccurate text of Cod. S. there are many erasures, as well as corrections, made by various hands not easily to be distinguished; a few of the latter seem to result from the collation of another MS. The MS. nearest allied to Cod. S. is one of the fourteenth or perhaps the thirteenth century, which frequently exhibits the readings of Cod. S. that have become corrupted in later copies. For example, this MS. has not *oro*[5] vi. 12, nor *orauit*[6] vii. 36, nor *uenerunt* vii. 38, the first of which has

---

[1] Among the later MSS. examined by me, C. 6, L. 7, O. 3, 6, and W. have *sequenti precedente*, C. 12 has only *sequenti*.

[2] I have found *ex parte* in C. 10, 11, H. and L. 5.

[3] *Et pauor* is also the reading of C. 6, 12, O. 3,

and W., and *ut pauor* of L. 7. Another variant is *et uita nostra pauor*, found in C. 10, 11, and L. 5.

[4] See below, p. 32.

[5] The word *oro* is omitted in C. 3, 9, H., L. 3, 4, O. 1.

[6] The absence of a verb in Cod. S. is now explained by the recovery of the lost part of the

been added in many, and the second and third in all other copies, in order to complete the sense; it stands alone with Cod. S. in having all the words in the following group[1]: *uoluptate* iii. 8, *delinqui* iii. 31, *ualidis* vii. 42, *auis* xi. 19 (corrupted in others to *aliis, alis, illis*). The original of the MS. in question was copied from Cod. S. before some of the corrections had been inserted, and so we find there *dedit* iii. 5 (comp. the Syr. and Aeth.), as also in Cod. S. pr. m., for *dedisti*[2] is from a second hand. In iv. 17 this MS. has *harene* and *eam* as Cod. S., where however the former has been altered to *harena*, the latter to *eum*. Again, in iv. 21 the *quae* before the last *super* is absent from this MS., in Cod. S. it has been added later. On the other hand, some corrections had been already introduced, e.g. in iii. 22, Cod. S. had originally *malum*, and in iii. 26 and iv. 4 *cor malum*, where in each case the adj. is altered to *malignum*, and this is the reading found in that MS. Other copies have introduced in iii. 26 the further corruption *corde maligno*."

"In attempting therefore to restore the earliest form of the Latin, we must always make Cod. S. our starting-point; all other MSS. which have the lacuna after vii. 35 are worthless. It is only an uncritical dilettantism that would construct a text, by balancing the readings of Cod. S. with the arbitrary variations of two or three MSS. which are copied from it. Cod. S. certainly offers no intelligible text, and yet it forms the only basis for conjecture."

From my own examination of Cod. S. and other MSS. I could bring forward many arguments of a like kind in support of the conclusion at which Prof. Gildemeister arrives. For instance, in ii. 40, Cod. S. has *respice* altered to *recipe;* the latter I have found in the majority of MSS., but the former is by no means uncommon[3]. In iii. 17, Cod. S. has *factus est* corrected to *factum est;* the latter is the usual reading in MSS.; the uncorrected form is retained in Codd. C. 6, O. 3, T. and W. (in C. 12 we find *factus es*). So *facit* has been altered to *fecit* in iii. 31, Cod. S.; the original reading is again represented by Codd. C. 6, 12, O. 3, T. and W., and the correction by the majority of MSS. The untenable construction *ut non decurrunt*, which Cod. S. presents in vi. 24, naturally gave rise to two readings, *et non decurrent*, C. 6, 12, L. 7, O. 3, T., W. and Vulg., and *ut*

---

chapter; the last word on the leaf cut out of this MS. was doubtless *rogauit*.

[1] I have not found a MS. with the readings of Cod. S. in all these passages, a considerable number however (C. 3, 4, 7, 8, 10, 11, H., L. 1, 2, 3, 6, O. 1, 2, 5, 6) have the word *uoluptate*; C. 1 has *delinqui*;

C. 1, 3, 9, H., L. 4, 9, O. 1, 6, have *pro ualidis*, and C. 10 has (not *auis*, but) *auibus*.

[2] See below, p. 25.

[3] *recipe* Codd. C. 1, 2, 4, 5, 6, 9, 10, 11, 12, 13, H., L. 1, 5, O. 1, 2, 3, 5, and W.; *respice* Codd. C. 7, 8, 14, L. 2, 4, 6, 7, O. 6, 7.

non decurrant, which proves to be correct and is found in most MSS.[1] Again, Cod. S. had originally *sed non in tempore non omnia...saluantur,* viii. 41, but the second *non* has been struck out; here also the uncorrected text is preserved in Codd. C. 6, 12, D., L. 7, O. 3, T. and W., the corrected text in most other MSS. A few verses lower down (viii. 45), Cod. S. has *tu enim creaturae misereris,* with *ae* added above the line after the first word; this is probably the source of the variations which are found in this passage, e. g. *tu enim creat. mis.* C. 5, 10, 11, O. 5, *tue enim creat. mis.* C. 1, 3, 4, 7, 8, 9, H., L. 9, O. 1. 2, 6, and *tu autem creaturae tuae misereris,* C. 2, 6, 12, D., L. 7, O. 3, T., W. and Vulg. In x. 20, the word *hunc,* which was left out by the transcriber of Cod. S., has been supplied on the margin; as there written it stands before *sermonem* (the first word of the line), but a slight mark is inserted to indicate that it has been omitted after that word; hence we meet with it in both positions, *hunc sermonem* in Codd. C. 2, 6, 12, D., L. 7, O. 3, T., W. and Vulg., and *sermonem hunc* in most of the MSS. I will now give an example of another kind, but one no less convincing: in xi. 32, *et dominabit qui inhabitant terram in ea* is the reading of Cod. S., but the Oriental versions alone (if we had no other evidence) are sufficient to prove that *terram* has crept in from the preceding clause (comp. the usual formula which occurs in verse 34, xii. 23, 24, and elsewhere); but this word once introduced through Cod. S. has, in spite of all efforts to rectify the construction, remained to this day a disturbing force in all MSS. and printed editions[2]. In xv. 36, the original reading in Cod. S. is *femur,* but the letter *r* is written with an upward flourish, so that at first sight it would be readily mistaken for an *f*[3]; to make the word in some sort intelligible, an *i* has been drawn through the *e,* and thus the strange reading *fimus* has passed into subsequent copies[4].

It seems superfluous to accumulate examples of this kind, yet the argument would be incomplete if I did not call attention to the lacunae as furnishing weighty evidence in determining the pedigree of MSS. Now wherever words have been omitted in Cod. S.,

---

[1] In vi. 34, Cod. S. has *ut non properas,* which has been emended in like manner to *ut non properes.* The reading, *et non properes,* retained by modern editors from the Vulg., seems not to be countenanced by the MSS.

[2] C. 10 has *et dominabantur qui inhabitant terram in ea,* but the effect of the insertion of *terram* has generally been to drive the words *in ea* from their position, as in Cod. T.: *et dominabitur in ea hiis qui habitant terram,* and they are similarly placed

after the principal verb in most Codices, as C. 2, 4—8, 11, 12, D., H., L. 7, O. 2, 3, 5, 7, and W., while in C. 3, 9, O. 1, they are expelled as a hindrance to the sense.

[3] A few verses lower down (xv. 45) there is a similar confusion between these two letters in the same MS.; hence the two variations, *constantes* in the Vulg., *constanter* in most MSS.

[4] In some early editions it is printed *fumus,* hence Coverdale's translation: *and the smoke of man unto yᵉ Camels lytter.*

they seem to have been lost for all subsequent MSS. To quote a few instances, in vii. 112 (42) the subject of *orauerunt* is wanting in Cod. S. and apparently in all later copies; Volckmar supplies it by the insertion of *ualidi*, which gives the sense, though, as we shall see, not the language of the original Latin. A comparison with the other versions will disclose important lacunae common to Cod. S. and later MSS. in the following passages: ix. 20, x. 60—xi. 1, xi. 2, and xiii. 22. In xii. 11, *quartum* has evidently dropped out after *regnum*, and so this indispensable epithet has ever since been absent from the Latin text. The Oriental versions point to the presence of *loquar* before *coram te* in xiv. 18; that word is not in Cod. S., nor have I detected it in any other MS. When an omission creates a void that may be felt, it is but natural that attempts should be made by copyists to fill it up; we have an instance of this in a passage already quoted, vii. 106 (36), where the removal of a leaf from Cod. S. has left the clause without its verb, and *orauit* has been supplied incorrectly, as we now know, in the MSS. that come after Cod. S. A more ambitious attempt to restore the text may be seen in the same chapter, verse 115 (45), where four words absent from Cod. S. are found inserted in later MSS. In this case, I think that the *neque* before *demergere* clearly indicated the loss of a clause, which was supplied ingeniously enough, but, to judge from independent witnesses, incorrectly by the words: *salvare eum qui periit.* It is in fact this tendency among transcribers to write what is clear and intelligible instead of what is doubtful or difficult to understand, which will explain many curious deviations of later copies from their prototype, Cod. S. To begin with an alteration manifestly incorrect: in ix. 17, Cod. S. has *et qualis agricola talis et atria;* the easy emendation of the last word (*area* for *atria*), proposed by Volckmar, seems not to have occurred to a scribe, and so *cultura* was boldly substituted, and is now the reading of most MSS.[1] So in xii. 32, the *infulcit* of Cod. S. reappears as *incutiet* in the MSS. and printed editions. In xvi. 10, *surgebit*, the reading of Cod. S., has been changed by later scribes to *pauebit* (the true word, as we shall afterwards see, is *horrebit*). It required no great critical acumen to replace *filii a potestate*, xv. 25, Cod. S., by *filii apostatae*[2], or *misereatur*, vii. 133 (63), Cod. S., by *miserator;* the change in the latter case proves that the key to the structure of the whole passage had been discovered, and prepares us for the further emendation of *muneribus*, vii. 135 (65), in Cod. S., to *munificus* in later MSS., which might otherwise have seemed beyond the range of a simple copyist. The reading *absolve*, in viii. 4, Cod. S. (retained in C. 10), is by a true instinct

---

[1] C. 10 retains *atria* from Cod. S.

[2] τέκνα ἀποστάται (Is. xxx. 1), not τέκνα ἀποστά-του as Hilg. p. 208.

changed to *absorbe* in most MSS. Sometimes a single Codex not rising above the dead level of ordinary transcripts surprises us with a happy emendation[1] of an error, which had apparently taken permanent possession of the text. Thus, in C. 5, instead of the long-familiar blunder, *et non significasti, nihil memini, quomodo...,* iii. 30, 31, we unexpectedly come on a reading which anticipates by six centuries the certain emendation of Van der Vlis, *et non significasti nihil nemini, quomodo...* Again, we might look long for any improvement on the reading, *quando plantasti terram,* iii. 4; Hilgenfeld assumes it to be correct in his reproduction of the Gk. ὅτε ἐφύτευσας τὴν γῆν, and disregards the consensus of the other versions in favour of an original ὅτε ἔπλασας τὴν γῆν; the natural equivalent to ἔπλασας is *plasmasti*[2], a reading which I have actually detected in two MSS. (L. 7 and O. 6). There are some corrections now generally accepted which seem to be of comparatively recent introduction, at any rate I have only noticed them in MSS. contemporary with the earliest printed text. To this class I would refer the change of *et si* to *et ipsi,* viii. 56, and of *initium per consummationem* to *initium habet pariter et consummationem,* ix. 5. The most striking alteration of this kind which I have observed is in viii. 44; in this verse the singular reading, *hic pater et filius homo,* to judge from the evidence before me, maintained its ground in the MSS. till the invention of printing, when it became recast in the form which, with but little variation, it has ever since retained: *sic perit et similiter homo.* At the same period a lacuna of long standing in vii. 113 (43) was filled up by the insertion of *et initium,* which the context suggests and the other translations confirm.

The investigation therefore of the sources of the present text forces us to the conclusion that many manuscript readings unhesitatingly adopted by editors can only be regarded as conjectures more or less ingenious, which must always be scrutinized with the greatest caution. In each case we are thrown back on the authority of

---

[1] On the other hand, the MSS. exhibit corruptions equally startling; these sometimes result from the tendency to substitute the known for the unknown, as *Armenii* xv. 30, C. 3, 4, 9, O. 5, for *Carmonii* Cod. S.; *Nazareth* xiii. 45, C. 10, for *Arzareth* (that mysterious land which, after having so long baffled critics, has been discovered by Dr. Schiller-Szinessy to be nothing more than *Terra alia,* comp. ver. 40, the ארץ אחרת of Deut. xxix. 27, stereotyped in all its vagueness as a proper noun. See the *Journal of Philology,* Vol. III. 1870). In a few cases the religious feelings of the scribe have given a colouring to the text, as *ut et ecclesiam timeant et trepidentur omnes* xv. 29, C. 10, for *ut etiam timeant...,* even to the violation of the laws of grammar and of nature, as *et mulieres* ET HERETICI *parient menstruatae monstra* v. 8, which I have found with this interpolation in no less than three MSS. (C. 7, 8, and L. 2).

[2] Another instance may be quoted to shew how liable these verbs are to be confounded: in viii. 14, for *plasmatus est* Cod. H. has *plantatus est.*

Cod. S., and with advantages to which a scribe of the middle ages could not aspire, such as the light to be derived from other ancient versions and from the researches of modern criticism, we must do our best to make the crooked straight and the rough places plain. But although the theory just propounded deprives us of the help which we might otherwise have expected from the later MSS., so many of which remain still unexamined, it will be some consolation to know that we shall not be left in hopeless dependence on Cod. S.; for Cod. A., which we have kept in abeyance during this discussion, not only restores to us the portion of the book which seemed irrevocably lost from the Latin, but, as we shall soon see, will henceforth be entitled to rank as a co-ordinate authority with Cod. S. in settling the text of this very difficult book.

The great similarity existing between these two MSS. will doubtless have been already remarked from the quotations in the preceding pages; this similarity can frequently be traced in the minutest details, both in the original and corrected readings. For example, in i. 36 Cod. A. supports Cod. S. in the reading *et memorabuntur antiquitatum eorum*[1]. The abrupt address in i. 38, *Et nunc, frater, aspice cum gloria et uide populum uenientem ab oriente*, is attended with many difficulties; by the easy substitution of *fr̄* for *fr̄*, the reading *superaspice* found its way into many later MSS.[2], yet, strange to say, *frater* is not the original reading of either of our oldest authorities, for Cod. S. has (pr. m.) *pater* (*pat̄*), but *p* has been erased and *fr* written above, while the reading of Cod. A., *partem* (*partē*), differs so little in appearance from the word as first written in Cod. S., that it may be taken for a confirmation of that reading[3]. In ii. 15 *mater, amplectere filios tuos, educa illos cum*

---

[1] So apparently in most MSS. Fritzsche indeed retains the Vulg. *et memorabuntur iniquitatum eorum*, but I have not observed this variation in copies written before the 15th century. The mutilated form, *iquitatum*, assigned to T. (*Zeitschr. d. Wissensch. Theol.* VII. 334, but quoted as *equitatum* in the edd. of Hilgenf. and Fritzsche), stands midway between the two readings.

[2] Further corrupted to *semper* in Cod. H.

[3] Our first impulse is to refer the *pater* here and in ii. 5, *ego autem te, pater, testem inuoco super matrem filiorum...*, to the same person, but who is that person? Is it Ezra? The 'Erra pater' indeed, of modern times, occurs to us (see Addenda), but we lack evidence of the early use of such a title, not to mention that it would be singularly incongruous

in an address from God to his prophet. Again, the language which immediately follows in ii. 6, 7, *ut des eis confusionem...dispergantur in gentes...*, looks certainly like a direct appeal to God himself. Or is it God the Father, thus addressed by the Son? It is true there is no formal introduction of Christ as a speaker, but echoes from his words meet us on every side. This explanation is well adapted to the context in ii. 5, and is there accepted by Hilgenfeld, but it will scarcely be regarded as admissible in i. 38. Can the reading in the latter passage have resulted from an error in translation? It has not been sufficiently recognized that the author of 4 Ezra i. ii. drew much of his phraseology from Baruch iv. v. Comp. e.g. ii. 2 with Bar. iv. 19, ii. 3 with Bar. iv. 11, 12, ii. 4 with Bar. iv. 17, 21, ii. 12

laetitia. Sicut columba confirma pedes eorum, the position given to *columba* naturally suggested the alteration to *columnam*[1], which has been adopted by Coverdale, 'make their fete as fast as a piler,' and has thus passed into the Geneva and Authorized versions; but that *columba* may be retained, without the unnatural association found in the Vulg., is proved by the text and interpunctuation common to both our MSS., *mater complectere filios tuos educam illos cum laetitia sicut columba, confirma pedes eorum*. The long-standing error, *imperasti populo*, iii. 4, for *imperasti pulueri*, is already in possession of the text in Cod. A. as well as in Cod. S. Their minute agreement in the next verse enables us to observe an intermediate stage in the transformation of *et dedit tibi* to *et dedisti*, for in both MSS. the letter *s* in *dedisti* is a later insertion[2].

Codd. A. and S. agree in the following readings: *casui* iii. 10 (the *i* is erased in Cod. A.), *derelinquas* altered in both to *derelinqueres* iii. 15, *et offerre tibi*[3] *in eodem tuas oblationes* iii. 24 (*eodem* altered to *eadem* in Cod. A.), *tribus impii* iv. 23 (*in* has been afterwards inserted before *tribus* in Cod. A.), *de ea* (for *dicam*) iv. 28 (so also Cod. T.); in the same verse Cod. A. has *districtio* (altered to *destructio*), Cod. S. *destrictio*[4]. Again, they agree in *tu enim festinas uaniter* (altered to *inaniter* in Cod. A.)

with Bar. v. 8; and so also the language of the verse in question is evidently derived from Bar. iv. 36, 37, Περίβλεψαι πρὸς ἀνατολάς, Ἱερουσαλήμ, καὶ ἴδε τὴν εὐφροσύνην τὴν παρὰ τοῦ θεοῦ σοι ἐρχομένην. ἰδοὺ ἔρχονται οἱ υἱοί σου οὓς ἐξαπέστειλας, ἔρχονται συνηγμένοι ἀπὸ ἀνατολῶν ἕως δυσμῶν τῷ ῥήματι τοῦ ἁγίου, χαίροντες τῇ τοῦ θεοῦ δόξῃ. *Circumspice, Ierusalem, ad orientem et uide...* Comp. also Bar. v. 5, 6. If we assume then that the word which stood in the original Greek of 4 Ezra i. 38 was περίβλεψαι, or rather περίβλεψον (the latter has hitherto been quoted as the reading of the Cod. Vat. in Bar. iv. 36, incorrectly as it appears, for περίβλεψε (= -αι) is the form given in the edition of Vercellone and Cozza, Rome, 1872), this compound might easily have been mistaken for πέρ βλέψον, which would at once account for the *pater aspice* of the Latin translator. To prove that the present Latin text exhibits a distorted image of the Greek, we need only compare the position of the next words, *cum gloria*, with the context in which μετὰ δόξης stands in Bar. v. 6.

B.

[1] C. 1 has *columpna* (without stop), C. 9 *sicut columnam, confirma*.

[2] With the text thus restored: *imperasti pulueri, et dedit tibi Adam corpus mortuum*, comp. *imperasti terrae ut crearet coram te iumenta et bestias et reptilia, et super his Adam*, vi. 53, 54.

[3] Such is the obvious division of the words in the *et offerr&ibi* of Cod. S. (comp. in the same MS. *ostender&ibi = ostendere tibi* iv. 3), but an early corrector by an excusable oversight read *et offerret ibi*, and consequently altered *et* to *ut*.

[4] This reading of Cod. S. has been known from the time of Sabatier, but it seems to have been regarded by critics either as too insignificant to notice, or, if quoted, merely as an eccentricity in the spelling of the word, which has been universally adopted in the text, *destructio*. The authority of Cod. A. will lead, I believe, to a re-consideration of the long-neglected *destrictio*, for it better keeps up the metaphor which is expressed by the other versions. The Lexicons give no examples of *destrictio* or of *districtio* in the sense here required;

cum et ipsum spiritum, nam excelsus pro multis[1] iv. 34, *uenit* iv. 35, *ponderaui* iv. 36, *prorogas* altered in both to *interrogas* iv. 52, *conculcauerunt qui* (for *conc. eum qui*) v. 29, *credebant* (for *non credebant*)[2] ibid., *aut* (for *an*) v. 33, *qui necdum* v. 36 (so also C. 10, 11, and Syr.), *uiuificauit* v. 45, *qui ante sed minores* (*s* on eras. in A.) *statu*[3] v. 52, *Initium* vi. 1, *decores* (orig. *-ris* A.) vi. 3, *et antequam aestimaretur camillum Sion*[4] vi. 4, *quaē* (pr. m.) vi. 23, *intuebatur* vi. 29, *turbatur* altered in both to *turbabatur* vi. 36, *odoramentis inuestigabiles* (*-lis* in Cod. S.)[5] vi. 44. A word, which appears to be *progenitum*, is erased before *saeculum* vi. 55, in Codd. A. and S. Both have *quam* vii. 20 (*quā* altered to *quō* in Cod. A.), *incorruptibile* altered in both to *corruptibile* vii. 111 (41), *Et nouem mensibus patitur tua plasmatio tuae creaturae quae in eo creata est*, viii. 8, a passage which contains two anomalies of construction, apparently derived from the original. Comp. the Gk. of Hilgenfeld, καὶ ἐννέα μῆνας ἀνέχεται τὸ πλάσμα σου τοῦ κτίσματος τοῦ ἐν αὐτῷ κτισθέντος. The following words found in the Vulg. are absent from both MSS., *et initium* vii. 113 (43), *irascaris* viii. 45 (comp. the Or. Verss.), *ut* viii. 49 (but added later in both, in Cod. A. before *plurimum*, in Cod. S. before *inter*), *et* (before *miserabiles*) viii. 50 (this is a step towards bringing out the right construction as found in the Syr. &c.), *mali* viii. 53 (not in the Or. Verss.), *est* (before *manifesta*) ix. 5, *casum* x. 9 (this word is not represented in the Or. Verss. and is evidently introduced to help the construction). Codd. A. and S. seem to stand alone in reading *nunc uitam* viii. 60 (*nunc* is dotted above in Cod. S.). In ix. 16 *sicut multiplicatur fluctus super*

---

but comp. the use of *distringo* in the Vulg., *Et fructus eius distringet*, Ezek. xvii. 9. *Destructio* was not the only attempt to emend the original, for we find *distinctio* in C. 6.

[1] Cod. S. has *pro multis* (not *permultis*). In Cod. A. q̄n̄m̄ has been struck out before *nam*, and *nam excelsus pro multis* altered to *ab excelso acceperis*.

[2] In Cod. A. a corrector has changed *quique* to *eos qui*, so that the verse may now be read thus: *Et conculcauerunt qui contradicebant sponsionibus tuis eos, qui tuis testamentis credebant*, which conforms to the construction in the Syr. and Æth. versions.

[3] In v. 54, Cod. A. has *minoris statutis* altered to *minores statu estis*, Cod. S. *minores statutis*.

[4] As a distinguished Oxford Professor has lately quoted (*Fors Clavigera*, Letter xlvii. Oct. 1874), without misgiving, our Authorized Version of this

passage, 'or ever the chimneys in Sion were hot,' I may remark that the textus receptus *et antequam aestuarent ̄camini in Sion* is utterly destitute of credit. The only two MSS. which have any authority agree in the reading which I have given above. *Camillum* is for *scamillum* 'foot-stool.' Rönsch. p. 94, gives only *scamillus*, though Acts vii. 49, Cod. Bezae, to which he refers, has *scamillum* in the nominative; so also Matt. v. 35, Cod. Clarom. (*scamellum*, Cod. Sang. comp. *scamello* Jac. ii. 3, Cod. Corb.). For the metaphor comp. Lam. ii. 1. *Aestimaretur* is no doubt corrupt, we require in its place some such word as *stabiliretur, firmaretur*, or, as Hilgenfeld proposes, *aedificaretur* (among the guesses in MSS. we find *edificarent (sic) camini* in C. 6).

[5] See Rönsch, p. 112. His conjecture that Cod. S. has *inuestigabilis* is correct, but unnecessary, since it does not appear that the form *ininuestigabilis* has ever, as he assumes, been ascribed to that MS.

guttam Vulg., we find the reading *multiplicat fructus*[1] in both MSS., the verb being here used intransitively in imitation of the Gk. πλεονάζει. Similarly in xiv. 16 *tantum multiplicabuntur super inhabitantes mala*, Vulg., the form *multiplicabunt* is found both in Cod. S. and in Cod. A. (pr. m.). A misunderstanding of this anomalous usage of the verb has led to the omission of *super* in ix. 16, Cod. A., and in xiv. 16, Cod. S. (supplied pr. m. in the latter case on the margin)[1]. In ix. 19 *moribus*[2] (for *mores*) is common to the two MSS. (comp. the other versions). Modern editors have without an exception retained the reading of the Vulg. *o domine*, TE *nobis ostendens ostensus es patribus nostris in deserto* ix. 29. This is doubtless one of the many instances found in our book, of a well-known Hebrew idiom[3], but the insertion of the acc. of the pronoun is not justified by a comparison of the analogous phrase, *reuelans reuelatus sum* xiv. 3. In fact *te* is one of those attempts at emendation which were introduced at the time of the first printed edition; Codd. A. and S. and apparently all MSS. before that date have IN *nobis*. In ix. 45 Cod. A. has *ancillae tuae* (altered to *ancillam tuam*), Cod. S. has *ancillæuae*. Both have *proditi* (not *perditi*) x. 22, as Ambrose also quotes it (Lib. I. *de Excess. Sat.*)[4], *Uox exiebat* xi. 10 ($\bar{n}$ stands above the line after *uox* in Cod. S.), and *toto* (not *tanto*) *tempore* xi. 16. In xi. 19, Cod. S. has *omnibus auis*, Cod. A. *omnibus auibus*[5]. The reading of Cod. A. in xi. 37 is *et audiui quomodo* (comp. the Syr., Æth. and Arm.), Cod. S. has the word *audiui* altered to *uidi* and so transmitted to the other MSS. Cod. A. agrees with Cod. S. and a large majority of

---

[1] In ix. 16, *multiplicat* C. 3, 9, 10, *multiplicatur fructus* C. 1. In xiv. 16, *multiplicabunt* C. 1, 10, om. *super* C. 3.

[2] *moribus* C. 9, 10.

[3] It occurs, for instance, in iii. 33, iv. 2, 13, 26, v. 45, vi. 38, vii. 5, 14, 21, 67, 75, viii. 15, ix. 1, 29 (bis), x. 32, xi. 45, xiv. 3, 29, and even in the chapters attached to the end, as xv. 9; in all these examples the inf. abs. is expressed by the Lat. participle; in a few cases we find the abl. of the subst. as vi. 14, 31-32, vii. 67, and once the gerund xvi. 65. There are occasional efforts to get rid of this foreign construction, most frequently by the rejection of the participial element, as in viii. 15, x. 32, xi. 45, xiv. 29 Vulg., and in vii. 5, C. 10. In vi. 14 all MSS. had been led astray by Cod. S., and the true reading was only restored by an emendation of Van der Vlis. In vi. 31-32 *auditu* is omitted in C. 6, but

preserved in most MSS.; in the Vulg. (and also in Cod. T.) it has been corrupted to *audiui*. Our English translators have generally given due force to this idiom, but not always; in v. 45, for instance, *quoniam uiuificans uiuificasti a te creatam creaturam in unum* is translated by Coverdale 'that thou lyuynge maker hast made the creature lyuynge at once,' and the influence of this rendering is felt in the Gen. and in the A. V. In ix. 29 Hilgenfeld's Gk. is based entirely on the faulty text of the Vulg., he claims indeed the support of the Syr. but ἡμῖν has no representative in that version, and the words ܕܚܘܝܬ ܐܢܬ ܠܢ would be the ordinary translation for φανερωθεὶς ἐφανερώθης, or rather ἀποκαλυφθεὶς ἀπεκαλύφθης.

[4] *proditi* has passed from Cod. S. into C. 3, 5, 11, D.

[5] *omnibus auibus* C. 10.

the MSS. in reading *mugiens* for *rugiens* xi. 37, and *mugientem* for *et rugientem* xii. 31[1]. Both Codices have *emittit* (altered to *emisit* in Cod. A.) and *fluctum* altered to *flatum* xiii. 10, *occurrentes* xiii. 18 (*-es* is erased in Cod. S.), *in hac* for *in haec* xiii. 20[2], *prae medium* xiv. 12 (*-um* altered to *-o* in Cod. A.). Cod. A. has *et in terram Sion* xiv. 31, Cod. S. has *et in terra Sion* (*in* having been inserted). Both have *plebi* (with *s* added at the end) xv. 1, *exultans* (altered to *exaltans* in Cod. S.) xv. 53[3]. In xvi. 33 the *oues* of Cod. S. has been altered to *homines* in later MSS., but here also Cod. A. takes its place by the side of Cod. S. with the reading *eo quod non transeat ouis per eam*. In xvi. 39, the words *cum parit* are absent from both MSS.[4] This list might be considerably extended, but I will now close it with a few passages, where I first recovered the true reading from Cod. A., but found, as soon as I had an opportunity of examining Cod. S., that in these points also the two MSS. originally coincided. There is a striking instance of this in iii. 7, where Cod. A. reads *et huic mandasti dilegentiam unam tuam, et praeteriuit eam*. The presence of *diligentiam*, that characteristic word in the Latin of the fourth of Esdras[5], and the harmony of the other versions, at once stamp this as the genuine text[6], while the reading of Cod. S....*diligere uiam tuam...*, transmitted to nearly all later MSS.[7] and accepted by all editors, bears every mark of an alteration made to simplify the language. If we examine Cod. S. more closely, we shall have ocular demonstration of the way in which this alteration was introduced, for the last letter of *diligere* is written on an erasure, and we can still decypher faint traces of

[1] C. 10 has *rugiens* xi. 37, but *mugientem* xii. 31.

[2] *in hac* C. 10.

[3] *exultans* C. 10.

[4] *cum parit* is not in C. 10.

[5] See below on vii. 37.

[6] With the passage thus restored compare the following extract quoted in the ' Pugio fidei' of Raymundus Martini, (pp. 674, 675): אר" יוסי הגלילי צא ולמד זכות מלך המשיח ושכרן של צדיקין מאדם הקדמוני שלא נצטווה אלא מצוה אחת בלא תעשה ועבר עליה ראה כמה מיתות נקנסו לו ולדורותיו... This is said to be taken from the Siphre; Edzardus, in his *Annotat.* (Wolf. Bibl. H. iv. 622) gives no other explanation than ' ex citat. Salom.' Wünsche, who borrows the quotation (*Die Leiden des Messias*, p. 65), adds to the reference ' S. 121.' But I have in vain searched for it in the Siphre. Dr. Schiller-Szinessy,

however, who kindly lent me his aid, has succeeded in finding a similar passage, not in the Siphre, but in the Siphra, xii. § 10 (ed. Weiss, Wien, 1862, fol. 27 a, col. 1), as well as in the Yalkut (Livorno, 1650, fol. 220 b, § 479), and in Rashi on Lev. v. 17, in all of which places the words that especially illustrate the point under discussion appear with some slight variations. But should this be really the source of Raymundus Martini's quotation, it may be here mentioned that in other respects there are material discrepancies, such as the absence of all Messianic application in these three authorities; a fact which it would be well for those to consider who continue to appeal to this extract as ' ein sehr klares und bestimmtes Zeugniss von dem Verdienste des Messias.'

[7] One variation may be noted, viz. *diligere mandata tua et praeteriuit ea*, Cod. H.

the termination *-tiam;* again it will be seen that *uiam* results from the erasure of the second stroke of the *n* in the original text *unam.* Cod. A. has *extincta* in viii. 53, and this (not *et tincta*) is also the reading of Cod. S. Chap. xiv. 11 stands thus in the two latest editions: *Duodecim enim partibus diuisum est saeculum, et transierunt eius decimam et dimidium decimae partis.* For *decimam,* Cod. A. has *decem iam,* and whatever difficulties still remain with regard to the calculation[1] in this and the following verse, the construction thus obtained is confessedly more natural, for the reading of the Vulg. *decima* is a step in this direction, and our English translators[2] by a happy instinct have expressed the very words of Cod. A. The reading *Xam* has been invariably assigned to Cod. S., but looking at it in the light thrown on the passage by Cod. A. we at once detect the erasure of an *i* before the *a,* so that here again the two MSS. concur. In the example which I will now adduce, the correct expansion of an abbreviation will bring the two MSS. into unison. In ix. 19 Fritzsche edits: *tunc enim erat nemo,* and remarks *pro 'nemo' in Codd. nescio quo errore legitur 'quisque,'* but Cod. S., which is the source of this reading, has *quisq;* this contraction must here stand for *quisquam*[3], which is the reading of Cod. A.; but adopting this, we must proceed a step further, and, substituting *nec* for *tunc,* restore the whole passage thus: *et nemo contradixit mihi, nec enim erat quisquam* (οὐδὲ γὰρ ἦν οὐδείς)[4]. In xiii. 48—49 it is only a faulty interpunctuation that keeps the two MSS. apart. Cod. A. reads correctly ...*intra terminum meum sanctum; erit ergo...* The very same words stand in Cod. S.; but the insertion of a stop (.;) before, instead of after, *sanctum* (sc̄m) has produced an impression, shared alike by ancient copyists and modern collators, that the reading of that MS. is ...*intra terminum meum. Factum erit ergo...*

It would however be a mistake to conclude from this long catalogue of resemblances that in Cod. A. we have little more than a repetition of the text given in Cod. S. Quite as many divergences in reading[5] might be quoted to shew that,

---

[1] In C. 10 there is an attempt to remove this numerical confusion by reading *undecimae* for *decimae* in both verses.

[2] Coverdale's translation is ' For the tyme is deuyded in to twolue partes, and ten partes of it are gone all ready, and half of the tenth parte.' Similarly the Gen. and A. V.

[3] C. 11 preserves the abbreviation from Cod. S. In C. 10 there is a fair attempt at emendation, *tunc non erat quisquam.*

[4] In xiii. 52, *sic non poterit quisque super terram uidere...*Cod. S. has the same contraction, and Cod. A. has *quisquam* (after *terram*). The requirements of the construction have introduced the word *quisquam* into several MSS., as C. 1, 3, 4, 5, 7, 8, 9, 11, D.

[5] Many specimens of readings peculiar to Cod. A. may be gathered from these pages; a few more are here subjoined, some of which may prevent us from overestimating the value of that authority: *crescunt*

however close the relationship between the two MSS., they are yet perfectly independent of each other. In proof of this we may appeal to the fact that in several places, where there is a lacuna in Cod. S., the Latin text is found complete in Cod. A. For instance, this MS. first supplies us with the correct form of the subject in vii. 112 (42): *propter hoc orauerunt* QUI POTUERUNT *pro inualidis.* The omission as usual must be referred to homœotel.[1] Cod. A. first fills up the gap in ix. 20, thus:

Et consideraui saeculum meum, ET ECCE PERDITUM ERAT ET ORBEM MEUM, *et ecce erat periculum.*

Comp. the Syr. It is true that here the missing words may have stood originally in Cod. S., for a line has been erased in this place, but I think that the erasure will be best accounted for by supposing that in the confusion arising from the similarity of the clauses, some words were by mistake written twice. In ix. 21 Cod. S. has *et peperci eis ualde;* but *ualde* does not fall in with the spirit of the next words, *et saluaui mihi acinum de butru.* From Cod. A. we recover the lost particle *et peperci eis* UIX *ualde*[2]. Through the same authority another passage which has been curtailed by a common oversight will be henceforth restored to its proper proportions: *Et dormiui illam noctem et aliam sicut* PRAECEPIT MIHI. ET FACTUM EST SECUNDA NOCTE ET ALIA SICUT *dixerat mihi et uidi somnium,* x. 60, xi. 1. And, lastly, the kingdom which appeared to Daniel is described more explicitly in Cod. A. as *regnum* QUARTUM xii. 11. Enough has been said to prove the independent position which Cod. A. occupies, but it may still be asked whether there are absolutely no readings that have possibly filtered through, if not from Cod. A. at least from some kindred MS. now lost, into one or other of the later copies. I confess that at first there were some

---

for *creuerunt* i. 6, *Testamentum* for *sacramentum* ii. 7, *populo* for *pupillo* ii. 20, *secreta noctu* iii. 14, *tremefecisti* iii. 18, *caelum* for *saeculum* iii. 18, *faciunt Babylonii* iii. 31, *sicut haec Jakob* iii. 32, *flatus* iv. 5, *tecum cogita altiss*^*imi* *scientiam non...* iv. 10, *mensura mensuraui saecula et tempora* iv. 37, *quem considerasti* v. 27, *defectionem* for *defatigationem* v. 35, *et uiuent et seruabuntur* vi. 21, *Leuitam* vi. 49, *Leuitae* vi. 52, *altum et spatiosum et inmensum* vii. 3, *si enim declinaueris* viii. 32, *munitio* for *motio* ix. 3, *tibi experienda* x. 49, *orationem* for *deprecationem* xiii. 14, *qui*^*d* *in corde aut in profundo maris* ^*sii*sic...xiii. 52,...*ei secreta multa temporum* xiv. 5.

[1] In verse 115 (45) of this chapter, *saluare eum qui periit* is absent from both MSS., being, as before stated, a conjectural insertion introduced into subsequent copies. But in Cod. A. the words *neq. euerterit· qui uictus fuerat,* which have been added on the margin to be attached to the end of the verse, may preserve some element of the original reading; for *uictus fuerat* comes nearer to the Syr. and Æth. versions than the *periit* of later MSS.

[2] Similarly the Syr. and Æth. versions. In the Arab. the reading of the two MSS. is not (as Ewald edits) فعطفت بوجهى, but فعطفت بوجعى.

isolated cases which perplexed me, where the bulk of the MSS. seemed to agree with Cod. A. and not with Cod. S.[1]; a subsequent collation however of the latter MS. and a careful attention to the erasures served to dispel these difficulties. Yet still it would be possible to draw up a pretty long list of readings that are found in Cod. A. and other MSS., but not in Cod. S. I believe that all of these will prove on examination to be mere accidental coincidences to be explained by the ordinary tendencies that produce fluctuations in the text[2].

[1] The following readings ascribed to Cod. S. would be clearly incompatible with the theory that all later MSS. may be traced back to this source alone:

unde sit　　iv. 4 S. Vulg., *quare* A. and the later
　　　　　　　　　　　　　　　　　　　MSS.
diebus tantis vi. 28 „　„ *tantis temporibus* „　„
ipsum　xiii. 58 „　„ *tempora*　　　　„　„

I find however in each of these places that Cod. S. really agrees, not with the Vulg., but with Cod. A. and the rest of the MSS. In vii. 18 the insertion of *in fine* (which Hilgenf. adopts for his text) seems to separate Cod. S., not only from all other MSS., but also from the Vulg. The error in this case arose simply from not observing the difference of type in the foot-note of Sabatier, where he refers to the last word in the verse: ' MS. Sangerm. in fine *non viderunt*, pro *non videbunt*.' My collation of Cod. S. has in several other points brought out more clearly the relation in which that MS. stands to the rest, as the following corrections will shew:

Achiae i. 2, *ex eo* iii. 21, *babillonem* (*m* erased) iii. 28, *in saeculum* iii. 34, *per nomina inuenies* iii. 36, *potest* iv. 9 (hence *potest* C. 4, 5, 10, 11; *potes* C. 1, 3, 7, 8, 9, H.), *flamma, et uidi* iv. 48, *superauerant* iv. 49 (so C. 3, 4, 5, &c.), *fortitudinem* v. 55, *uisitas* v. 56, *aut sequentis* vi. 7, *quo apparerent tunc* vi. 40 (*tunc* is in C. 3, 4, 5, &c. and in A.), *creauit* altered to *certauit* vii. 127 (57) (*creauit* C. 3, 9), *prophetes* viii. 5 (so C. 3, 5, 7, 8, 9, &c.), *fructum* viii. 10, *quae* (altered to *qui*) *fecit* viii. 60, *mense* ix. 19, *glorificamini* ix. 31 (so C. 5, 9, H.), *cum timore* x. 26, *cōmoueretur* altered to *comederetur* x. 26 (the latter in C. 3, 9, 10), *inhabitabunt* xi. 40, om. *tua* xi. 43 (so C. 3, 5, &c.), *renouabit* xii. 23, *manducabam* xii. 51, om. *ut* xiii. 32, om. *cum* xiii. 46, *superant* xiv. 12, *qui eam exterruerunt* xv. 45,

p̄da xv. 63.

[2] This will be best illustrated by a few characteristic examples: *Latilibus* ii. 31 S., *latibŏlis* A., *latibulis* C. 1, 3, 4, 5, &c. (We find two attempts to emend the above error of Cod. S.: (1) *lateribus* L. 7, T., Vulg., and (2) *latibulis* C. 1, 3, 4, 5, &c. The latter was successful); *uoluptate* iii. 8 S., C. 3, 4, 10, 11, &c., *uoluntate* A., C. 5, 12, L. 4, 7, W. (These words constantly interchange); *seruare* iii. 36 S., C. 7, 8, *seruasse* A., C. 1, 2, 3, 4, &c., Vulg.; *qui inuocatus est* iv. 25 S. and most MSS., *quod inuocatum est* A., C. 10, Vulg.; *Hieremihel archangelus* iv. 36 S., *Iheremiel angelus* C. 5, *Ieremiel archangelus* L. 1, 2, 3, 4, Vulg., *archangelus Oriel* A., *Uriel archang.* C. 10, *Urihel archang.* C. 6, *Huriel archang.* C. 7, 8, L. 7. (Instead of *Hieremihel*, the name of the angel who replies to the souls of the righteous, which occurs nowhere else in the book, it was natural for a scribe to write *Uriel*, the name of the angel then speaking with Ezra; this substitution was made several times independently, e.g. in Cod. A., in some later MSS., and also in Arab.[2]); *egressos* v. 5 S., *et gressus* A. and most MSS.; *Spalthihel* v. 16 S., *Phalthiel* A., C. 4, L. 1; *sicut in nouissimorum...nec in priorum* v. 42 S., *sicut non nouiss....nec priorum* A. and most MSS.; *nunc* vii. 132 (62) S., C. 1, 3, 4, 5, &c., om. *nunc* A., C. 2, Vulg.; *thesaurus mortalitatis* viii. 54 S., *thesaurus inmortalitatis* A. and the other MSS.; *habitatio in Hierusalem* x. 47 S., similarly C. 2, Vulg., om. *in* A., C. 1, 3, 4, 5, &c. (comp. *ruina Hierusalem* x. 48); *temporum finem et temporum nouissima* xii. 9 S. &c., *finem et temporum* omitted through homœot. in A., C. 2, Vulg.; *esca* xii. 51 S., C. 1, 3, 4, 5, &c., *mihi aesca* A., *mihi esca* C. 7, *esca mihi* Vulg.; *absconsa in absconsis certa; hic nouit adinuentionem uestram* xvi. 63, 64 S., *terrae* for *certa* D., T.,

I will now bring forward a few more noteworthy readings of Cod. A., some of which throw a new and unexpected light on dark passages of the Latin version.

The MSS. seem to be nearly equally divided between the readings *et in ira agebant* and *et mira agebant* in iii. 8[1]. A similar parallelism in Gen. xlix. 6 might be alleged in favour of the former, but to this the other versions are opposed; they rather support the reading of Cod. A., *et impie agebant*, which is also more in accordance with the style of the translation. Comp. iii. 30, vii. 18, viii. 35. Perhaps no word in the book has been more perplexing to editors than *exterius*, which is the reading of Cod. S. and most other copies in the following passage: *et iam exterius corrupto saeculo* iv. 11. Among the few variations may be noted *et iam ex te corrupto saeculo* L. 7 (comp. T.). Volckmar thought that the original Gk. would have been best rendered by *obnoxius;* Hilgenfeld substitutes his own emendation: *et qui existis in corrupto saeculo;* Fritzsche, regarding the Latin as hopelessly corrupt, has relegated it to a foot-note. Cod. A. solves the difficulty by reading *exterritus*, i.e. *exteritus*, ‘worn out,’ ‘corrupted’ (see above, p. 15, l. 15). This form of the participle of *extero* is not recognised in Lexicons, but we have on the one hand, the perf. *exteruerunt*, as we must read it, in xv. 45, (comp. *conterui* Rönsch, p. 287, and J. N. Ott, *Neue Jahrbücher f. Philologie und Paedagogik*, Leipzig, 1874, p. 792), and on the other, the substantive *exteritionem*[2] xv. 39, Cod. S. In iv. 29, Cod. A. has *si ergo non mensum fuerit quod seminatum est.* The corrected reading *non messum* at once commends itself to us by its agreement with the Syr. and Æth., while the original form *non mensum* explains the curious reading in Cod. S. ·*nom suū*, which has produced a large crop of conjectures[3]. Instead of ...*impleatur iustorum ****** areae* iv. 39 Cod. S., we have in Cod. A. ...*impleatur iustorum area*[4], as Hilgenfeld suggests. *Si non queris* (not *quaris*) is the reading of Cod. S. in vii. 9; since it is quite unintelligible in the context in which it stands, it has passed through various transformations in the MSS., e.g., *si non quis* C. 9, 10, 11,

---

Vulg., *in absconsis absconsa. certe hic nouit adin. u. A., absconsa in absconsis. certe hic nouit adin. u.* C. 3, 4, 5, 7, 8, 10, &c. (But it must be noted (1) that in Cod. S. a point has been erased before *certa*, and (2) that the order of the words preceding *certe* is different in Cod. A.).

[1] *et in ira agebant* S., C. 4, 5, 6, 9, H., L. 1, 2, 3, 4, 6, 7, O. 1, 3, D.; *et mira agebant* C. 1, 2, 3, 7, 8, 10, 11, 12, L. 5, O. 2, 5, 6, T., W., Vulg.

[2] So also C. 9, 10, C. 11 (on. marg.), *exterritio-*

nem C. 3, 7, 8, *exercitationem* C. 11 (in text), H.; *extritionem* was the original reading of Cod. A., but it has been converted by the insertion of -*ca*- to *extricationem*.

[3] As *non inuersum* T., Vulg.; *non in usum* C. 6, O. 3, *non usum* C. 5; *non euulsum* C. 3, 4, 7, 8, 9, 10, 11, D., L. 2, 3, 4, 5, O. 1, 2, 5, *non inuulsum* L. 1, *non emissum* O. 7.

[4] This is also the reading of Cod. H.

L. 9, *si nunquam* C. 3, 6, and so Vulg., *si nusquam* D., *si non* C. 4, 5, 7, 8, H., L. 1, 2, *sine* C. 1. Now Cod. A. has the same reading as that just quoted from Cod. S., but over queris (thus deleted) the word *heres* has been written, so that the passage may now be read *si non haeres antepositum periculum pertransierit, quomodo accipiet haereditatem suam?*, which is confirmed by the Syriac. The reading of the Vulg. in vii. 116 (46) *...sermo meus primus et nouissimus* must have resulted from an attempt to improve the text, for the words *...et non nouissimus* were transmitted by Cod. S. to the later MSS. This emendation in the Vulg. turns out in this instance to be correct, for it is supported not only by the Syr., Æth., and Arab., but also by Cod. A. Again, this MS. stamps with its authority the emendation of Hilgenfeld, *solum modicum* (for *solum modum* in Cod. S.) viii. 5, and that of Van der Vlis, *in nouissimis diebus* (for *a nouissimis diebus* in Cod. S.) x. 59. The reading *non comparuit*, also suggested by the scholar just mentioned, emerges from the confused text of Cod. A. in xii. 2 (-*uit* being written over an erasure). In xii. 31 the original reading of Cod. A. is *loquentem ad aquilam et arguentem eam iniustitias ipsius*[1] (for *...eas iniustitias ipsius*, Cod. S.). In xii. 35 Cod. A. alone has the correct reading, *et haec interpretatio eius* (for *et haec interpretationes* Cod. S.), and in xiii. 17 *erunt* (for *erant*, Cod. S.). The preposition (*in*) before *pericula*, xiii. 19, is absent from Cod. A.; its presence in Cod. S. has effected the change of *uiderunt* to *uenerunt* in the later MSS. In xiii. 40, Cod. A. has *haec sunt uiii tribus*[2], but *...decem...*, the reading of Cod. S., has been written above. Cod. A. stands alone among the MSS. in reading *interpretationes quas audisti* xiv. 8, as the other versions require, instead of *...quas tu uidisti* Cod. S. In xv. 29, *et exient nationes draconum Arabum...et sic flatus eorum...fertur super terram*, we find in Cod. A. an important variation for *sic flatus*, viz. *sibilatus*[3]. The word *contentio*, xv. 33, has been accepted by editors solely on the authority of later MSS., for Cod. S. has *constantia*; in Cod. A. the passage stands thus: *et inconstabilitio regno*

---

[1] So also C. 7, 8. (This is another illustration of agreement between Cod. A. and some of the later MSS.) Various attempts have been made to obviate the unusual construction of the verb, e.g. *arguentem eam et iniustitias ipsius* C. 3, 5, 9, 11, D., T., Vulg., *arguentem eam iniusticiis ipsius* C. 10, *arguentem iniustitias eius* H., and in Cod. A. *eam* has been expunged by a corrector. In the next verse we have an instance of *arguo* with two accusatives, *et impietates ipsorum arguet illos*, Cod. S.,

and again in xiii. 37 Cod. A., S. and Vulg.; comp. Plaut. *Men.* v. 5. 37, Caecilius Stat. l. 149 (*Comic. Rom. Fragm.* ed. O. Ribbeck), and Prov. xxviii. 23, in the Old Lat. Speculum, *qui arguit hominem uias suas* (Mai, *Nov. Patr. Bibl.* I. 2, p. 45).

[2] The Æth. has also nine tribes; in the Syr. and Arab. the number is nine and a half.

[3] The only example of this word given in the Lexicons is from Caelius Aurel. *de Morb. Acut.* II. 27, *accedente spirationis persecutione cum quodam*

illorum. The text of xv. 51 is: *Infirmaberis. .ut non possint te suscipere potentes et amatores* Vulg., but for *possint te,* Cod. S. has *possituos,* and Cod. A. *possintuos,* but with the letter *s* written over ...*nt* erased; we may therefore venture to restore the passage thus: *ut non possis tuos suscipere potentes et amatores.* For *surgebit* xvi. 10, Cod. S., we read in Cod. A. *horrebit.*

In a short passage of the book we get a glimpse of the Latin text of a somewhat earlier period, for the Prayer of Ezra (viii. 20—36) has been handed down as an extract in a few MSS. of the Bible, the oldest of which is anterior to Cod. S., e. g. in the Cod. Vatican. reginae Sueciae num. 11, Saec. VIII. (= Cod. Vat.), in the Bibl. Ecclesiae Aniciensis Velaunorum, Saec. IX. (= Cod. Colb.), both collated by Sabatier, in a MS. of the Latin Bible in the Univ. Library of Jena, Saec. XIV. (= Cod. Jen.), collated by Hilgenfeld, in a MS. of Trin. Coll. Dubl., Saec. XIV. (= Cod. Δ.), and in a Bodl. MS., Saec. XV. (= Cod. O. 8), as well as in some other biblical MSS., which I shall hereafter notice; it also occurs in the Mozarabic Liturgy[1]. Now Cod. A., although maintaining in these verses its close connexion with Cod. S., yet in a few instances rather reflects the text transmitted by the above authorities; thus we have *qui habitas in aeternum* viii. 20, Vat., Moz., Colb., Jen., Δ., O. 8, *qui habitas in saeculum* Cod. A., comp. the Syr. and Æth., while Cod. S. reads *qui inhabitas saeculum,* and in viii. 28 *qui ex uoluntate tuum timorem cognouerunt,* Colb., Jen., O. 8, and Moz. (ed. Migne), *qui ex uoluntate; tuum timorem cogn.* Cod. A., comp. the Syr., Æth., and Arab., ...*ex uoluntate tuam timorem...* stands in Cod. S. and has naturally led to ...*ex uoluntate tua timorem...* in the copies made from it. In viii. 29, Vat., Colb., Jen., Δ., O. 8, as well as Moz. (ed. Migne), have *pecorum,* which is also the reading of Cod. A., whereas *pecudum* is the reading of Cod. S. In viii. 30, Vat., Colb., Moz. (as given correctly by Sabatier), Jen., O. 8, and Cod. A. have *sunt iudicati,* Cod. S. has *iudicati sunt* (scarcely *ludicati...,* for the first letter is more probably a lengthened '*i*')[2].

sibilatu uehementi, atque aspero.

[1] *Liturgia Mozarabica,* Vol. II., *Breviarum Gothicum,* Cant. LXI. p. 878 (Migne, *Patrologia Lat.* Tom. LXXXVI.). It is singular that the Abbé Le Hir searched in vain for this quotation (*Études Bibliques,* I. p. 141); he was naturally puzzled at the reference given by Volckmar ('Missale Romanum Mozarabicum, missa in feria post Pentecosten p. 136' *D. 4ᵗᵉ Buch Ezra,* p. 273), but a little consideration might have enabled him to see a confused combina-

tion of two distinct works in this 'titre bizarre,' viz. the *Miss. Rom.,* where chap. ii. 36, 37 is quoted, as Basnage points out (comp. Fabricius, *Cod. Pseudep. V. T.* Ed. 2, II. p. 191), and the *Brev. Mozarab.,* which contains the long quotation from ch. viii.

[2] In verse 33 we read, *iusti enim* Colb., Jen., Δ., O. 8, *iustus* (altered to -*ti*) *enim* Cod. A., while *iusti* alone is assigned to Cod. S., but the reading of this MS. was rather *iustus* or *iustis* (altered to *iusti*) followed by *enim* (now erased).

It is however in chapters xv. and xvi., which together form the 5th book of Esdras in the majority of MSS., that the text of Cod. A. differs most widely from that of Cod. S.; as an example we may compare xvi. 20—23 according to the two recensions:

Cod. A.

20 *Ecce famis plaga dimissa est, et tribulatio eius · tāquam mastix; castigatio in disciplina.*

21 *Et super his omnibus non se auertent ab iniquitatibus suis nec super has plagas · memorantur sempiterna;*

22 *Ecce erit annonae uilitas in breui super terram ut putent sibi esse directam pacem, tunc superflorescent mala super terram gladius et famis* (altered to -es).

23 *Et aperiant* (altered to *aporient*) *uitam super terram, et gladius dispersit* (altered to *disperdet*) *quae superauerint a fame.*

Cod. S.

20 *Ecce famis* (altered to -es) *et plaga et tribulatio et angustia, missa sunt flagella in emendatione.*

21 *Et in his omnibus se non conuertent ab iniquitatibus suis, neque flagellorum memores erunt semper.*

22 *Ecce erit annonae uilitas super terram, sic ut putent sibi esse directam pacem, et tunc germinabunt mala super terram, gladius famis* (altered to -es) *et magna confusio.*

23 *A fame enim plurimi qui inhabitant terram interient, et gladius perdet caeteros* (*ceteros* written above) *qui superauerint a fame.*

Again, a few verses lower down we have,

Cod. A.

30 *Quemadmodum relinquentur* (altered to -*quuntur*) *in oliueto tres uel quattuor oliuae,*

31 *Aut sicut in uinia* (altered to -*ea*) *uindimiata* (altered to -*dem*-): *& subremanet racemus patens · ab scrutantibus uindimiam* (altered to -*dem*-) *diligent* (two letters erased at end).

32 *Sic remanebunt...*

Cod. S.

30 *Quemadmodum relinquentur in oliueto et singulis arboribus tres aut quatuor oliuae,*

31 *Aut sicut in uinea uindemiata racimi* (altered to -ce-) *relinquentur ab his
qui diligenter uineam scrutantur.*

32 *Sic relinquentur...*

In these two chapters we have no Oriental version to assist us in the criticism
of the Latin text, and therefore quotations from early writers would be here especially
welcome, yet hitherto one only has been pointed out by editors, viz. a short citation
from xvi. 60 by Ambrose[1]; but some centuries before the date of our two oldest MSS.
several verses had been quoted from 5 Esdr. (= 4 Esdr. xv., xvi.) by a writer of our own
country[2]. It is a curious fact that the editors of Gildas have from time to time called
attention to the peculiar text of these extracts[3], without attracting the notice of a
single writer on this book of Ezra. I now give in full the quotations in Gildas,
and subjoin the passages as they stand in Cod. A., and in Cod. S. A comparison of
these seems to shew that in Cod. A. we have at last discovered the recension of the
text which was used by Gildas.

Gild. Epist.

Quid praeterea beatus Esdras propheta ille bibliotheca legis
xv. 21 *minatus sit attendite, hoc modo disceptans: 'Haec dicit*

---

[1] *Non utique de hoc tecto dicit, sed de illo: extendit caelum sicut cameram,* Epist. xxix. (ed. Bened.
Tom. ii. col. 909). This is evidently borrowed from
4 Esdr. xvi. 60, *qui extendit caelum quasi cameram,*
and not from a somewhat similar passage in Is. xl.
22, which is thus cited by Ambrose: *qui statuit
caelum ut cameram,* Hexaem. vi. § 2 (Tom. i.
col. 116).

[2] In the so-called 'Epistola' of Gildas, generally
ascribed to the middle of the sixth century. Thos.
Wright thinks, that it was rather the work of an
Anglo-Saxon, or foreign priest, of the seventh century (*Biogr. Brit. Lit.* p. 128), and his opinion is
adopted by H. Morley (*English writers, The writers
before Chaucer,* p. 219), but the earlier date is stre-

nuously defended by Dr. Guest (*Proceedings of the
Archaeological Institute,* 'Salisbury Vol.,' 1849,
p. 35).

[3] ' Haec Esdrae testimonia nonnihil etiam dif-
ferunt a uulgata lectione.' Gild. ed. Joan. Josseli-
nus, fol. 52 vers., A.D. 1568. The latest editor, the
Rev. A. W. Haddan, describes the passage from
chap. xvi. as ' Vet. Lat. ap. Vulg., with considerable
variations,' but his attempt to account for these
variations is not satisfactory: ' Gildas also quotes...
2 Esdras (16 verses), in the Old Latin retained in
V. but corrected by the Greek.' (*Councils and
Ecclesiastical Documents relating to Great Britain
and Ireland,* ed. by A. W. Haddan and W. Stubbs,
Vol. i. pp. 70, 185, A.D. 1869.)

22 *Dominus meus: Non parcet dextera mea super peccantes,*
nec cessabit romphaea super effundentes sanguinem innocuum
23 *super terram. Exibit ignis ab ira mea, et devorabit funda-*
24 *menta terrae et peccatores quasi stramen incensum. Uae eis*
25 *qui peccant, et non observant mandata mea, dicit Dominus,*
non parcam illis. Discedite filii apostatae, et nolite contami-
26 *nare sanctificationem meam. Nouit Deus qui peccant in eum,*
27 *propterea tradet eos in mortem, et in occisionem. Jam enim*
uenerunt super orbem terrarum mala multa.'

Various readings from Cod. B. (=Dd. I. 17, Univ. Library, Cambridge)[1].

22. *pareet* B. *romphea* B. 23. *terre* B. 24. *Ue* B. 26. *peccauit* B.

5 ESDR.

COD. A.[2]

xv. 21, 22   *Haec dicit d̄n̄s d̄s̄; non par-*
cet dextera mea sup peccan-*
tes ✓ nec cessauit rumphea
sup effundentes sanguinem in-
23   *nocuum sup terrā, & exiit ig-*
nis ab ira eius ⤴ & deuorauit fun-
damenta terrae · & peccatores
24   *quasi stramen incensum, Uae*
hiis qui peccant ⤴ et non obser-
uant mandata mea · dicit d̄n̄s,
25   *Non parcā illis: discedite filii*
apostate : Nolite contaminare
26   *scīficationē meā. Nouit d̄s̄ qui*
peccant in *eū Propterea tra-*
det eos in mortem et in occisio

---

[1] This is still the only surviving MS. of Gildas, that can be appealed to for the extracts which I quote. Some fragments of the Cottonian MS. (Vitellius A. VI.), as Mr. E. M. Thompson has kindly informed me, escaped the fire, but these do not contain the quotations from 5 Esdras.

[2] In these extracts the text is printed line for line as it stands in Cod. A., and in Cod. S.

27 *nem ;   Jam   enim   uenerunt*
su͟p   orbem   terrarū   mala.

22. *cessauit* altered to *-bit.*

Cod. S.

xv. 21   *Haec   dicit   dn̄s   d̄s·;*

22 *Non   parcⱥ   dextera   mea   su͟p   peccato-*
res.   nec   cessabit   rumphea   su͟p
effundentes   sanguinem   innocuū   su͟p

23 *terram·;   & exíít   ignis   ab   ira   eius   & deuo-*
rauit   fundamenta   terrae .   & peccatores

24 *quasi   stramen   incensum·;   Uę   eis   qui   pec-*
cant.   & non   obseruant   mandata   mea · dicit

25 *dn̄s·; Non parcam illis·; discedite filii a potes-*
tate·;   nolite   contaminare   s̄cificationē   med̄.

26 *qm̄ nouit dn̄s oms qui de∗∗línqunt in illū.*
ᴄppterea   tradidit   eos   d̄s   in   mortē   & in   occi-

27 *sionem·; Jam   enim   uenerunt   su͟p   orbem*
terrarum   mala.

In the following quotation from the next chapter, the agreement between the text of Cod. A. and that given by Gildas is still more marked:

Gild. Epist.

xvi. 3, 4, 5 *Immissus est gladius uobis ignis, et quis est qui recutiet ea?*
6 *nunquid   recutiet   aliquis   leonem   esurientem   in   silua?   aut*
nunquid   extinguet   ignem   cum   stramen   incensum   fuerit?
8 *Dominus   Deus   mittet   mala,   et   quis   est   qui   recutiet   ea?*
9 *Et   exiet   ignis   ex   iracundia   eius,   et   quis   extinguet   eum?*
10 *Coruscabit,   et   quis   non   timebit?   tonabit   et   quis   non   horrebit?*
11 *Deus   cuncta   minabitur   et   quis   non   terrebitur?   A facie eius*
12 *tremet   terra   et   fundamenta   maris   fluctuantur   de   profundo.*

5, 6, S. *recuciet* B.   9. *exiet* B., *exibit* ed. Jossel.   *quis qui ext.* B.   10. *Thonabit* B.
12. *de superbo* B.

5 Esdr.

Cod. A.

xvi. 3   *In-*
misͦus est gladius uobis;
& quis est qui auertat

4   *eum ? inmissus ÷ uobis*
ignis. & quis ÷ qui extin-

5   *guat eū? inmiͦsa sunt uobis*
mala · & quis ÷ qui recu-

6   *ciǣ ea ? Numquid recu-*
tiǣ aliquis leonē esuri-
entem in silua ? Aut nū-
quid extinguit ignē cū
stramen incensū fuerit ?

7   *Aut numquid recutiǣ sagitā*
inmiͦsam a sagitario forte?

8   *D̄n̄s̄ d̄s̄ mittit mala · & quis*

9   *recuciet ea ? & exiet ignis*
& iracundia eius · & quis est

10 *qui extinguat eū ? curus-*
cabit · & quis nun timebit ?
tonabit & quis non horre-

11 *bit ? D̄n̄s̄ cōminatur · quis*
non conterretur ? A faciae

12 *eius · trèmǣ terra a funda-*
mento eius · mare fluctuat²
de ꝯpfundo.

4. *inmissus* altered to *immissus.*
6. *esurientem*, *s* apparently added above *es-* and then erased.
9. *exiet* altered to *exit.*
10. *curuscabit* altered to *corus-*; *nun* altered to *non.*
11. *conterretur*, *con* erased.
12. *tremet* altered to *tremit*; *fluctuat²* altered to *fluctuat.*

Cod. S.

xvi. 3   *Missus ē uob̄*

4 *gladius. & quis ē qui auertat illūḍ? Mis-*
  sus ē uobis ignis. & quis ē qui extinguat

5 *illūḍ? Missa sunt uobis mala & quis ē*

6 *qui repellat ea? Numquid repell&*
  aliquis leonem esurientē in silua? aut
  extinguat ignem in stipulam moxque

7 *coeperit ardere? Numquid aliquis*
  repellit sagittā a sagittario forti

8 *missā? Dn̄s d̄s mittit mala & quis re-*

9 *pellat éa? Exi& ignis ex iracundia ei'*

10 *et quis ē qui extinguat eum? corrus-*
  cabit & quis non timebit? tonabit.

11 *& quis non surgebit? Dn̄s comminabit²?*
  & quis non funditus conteritur a facie

12 *ipsius? Terra tremuit & fundam̄ta*
  eius. mare fluctuat² de profundo.

3, 4. *missus* altered to *inmissus* (bis); *illud* altered to *illum* (bis).
5. *missa* altered to *inmissa.*
6. *extinguat* altered to *-guet.*
7. *repellit* altered to *-let.*
8. *repellat* altered to *-let.*
10. *corruscabit,* the first 'r' partially erased.

With these extracts I bring to a close my remarks on the textual criticism of the 4th book of Ezra, and of the chapters attached to it in the Vulg. The MSS. which I have examined will be found tabulated at the end of this Introduction. None of those hitherto discovered in English libraries can be ascribed to a period earlier than the 13th century. The references scattered through the preceding pages will enable us to single out the more interesting specimens in the list: Codd. C. 6, 12, L. 7, O. 3, and W., for instance, are often grouped together as exhibiting, like Cod. T., the state of the text in Cod. S. before many corrections had been made. Cod. C. 10 and occasionally Cod. C. 11 have preserved some difficult readings, which have been replaced in most other MSS. by attempted emendations. Cod. H. also sometimes retains readings of this kind, though embedded in much that is late and corrupt. Codd. C. 2, L. 8 and O. 4 may be dismissed without further remark, for the text of our book, as given by them, was probably copied from a printed edition. As it would be worth while to form gradually a complete catalogue of those MSS. of the Lat. Bible which contain the 4th book of Ezra, I will insert among the Addenda a supplementary list of all that have come under my notice. I take this opportunity of thanking numerous correspondents who have kindly assisted me in the search, and of stating at the same time that I shall be happy to receive further information on the subject from those connected with public or private libraries.

The references to the books quoted by me will, I trust, be readily understood; by Hilgenf. I denote the 'Messias Judæorum, ed. A. Hilgenfeld, Lips. 1869.' For Old Latin forms and constructions I have constantly referred to Rönsch's 'Itala und Vulgata, ed. 2, Marburg, 1875,' and the illustrations given by me may generally be regarded as supplementing his articles. As the missing fragment must henceforth be incorporated in chap. vii., I have ventured to make the necessary readjustment in the numbering of the verses; the awkward device of interpolating a chap. (vi.) in the middle of chap. vii. can scarcely be maintained any longer. In reprinting the patristic references to chap. vii. 36—105, I have not deemed it superfluous to subjoin various readings from a few MSS. which came to hand[1].

I regret that, owing to the little leisure at my disposal, the publication of this work has been delayed longer than might have been expected. It only remains for me now to return my thanks to Prof. J. Gildemeister for the letter which he has kindly allowed me to publish, to the Rev. F. J. A. Hort for examining the first proof of my notes on the Fragment and furnishing me with a series of valuable suggestions, and to Prof. W. Wright, who has been ever ready to aid me with his sympathy and counsel. To Dr. Ignace Guidi I am under special obligation for his careful collation of two Arabic MSS. in the Vatican. I will give a short account of their contents in the Addenda, reserving for a future work the full use of these important materials. M. J. Garnier also has a claim on my gratitude for the facilities afforded me during my visits to the Bibliothèque Communale at Amiens.

---

[1] The way in which the oft-quoted passage from Jerome has been passed on from editor to editor forms one of the many literary curiosities connected with the history of this book of Ezra. Instead of ' et *proponis* mihi librum apocryphum......ubi scriptum est quod post mortem nullus pro aliis *audeat* deprecari,' Fabricius by a strange oversight printed ...*propinas*... and ...*gaudeat*...; his mistake reappeared in Laurence and even in Lücke (so far as he quotes the passage, *Versuch einer vollst. Einleitung in d. Offenb. des Joh.*), and has been repeated by Volckmar, Hilgenfeld, and Fritzsche.

LIST OF MSS.

AMIENS.

Á. = 10, Bibliothèque Communale.

PARIS.

S. = 'Cod. Sangerm.', 11505, fonds Lat., Bibliothèque Nationale.

CAMBRIDGE.

C. 1. = Ee. IV. 28, University Library.
C. 2. = Dd. VII. 5, „ „
C. 3. = O. 4. 5, St. Peter's College.
  (Chapters i. ii. are not in C. 3.)
C. 4. = O. 4. 6, „ „
C. 5. = 531 (ol. 601), Gonville and Caius College.
C. 6. = D. III. 47, St. Catharine's College.
C. 7. = 2. A. 3, Jesus College.
C. 8. = C. 24, St. John's College.
C. 9. = I. 28, „ „
C. 10. = 2. 1. 6, Emmanuel College.
C. 11. = Δ. 5. 11, Sidney Sussex College.
C. 12. = 7. E. 3, Fitzwilliam Museum.

C. 13. = Ee. I. 16, University Library.
C. 14. = L. V. 24, Magdalene College.
  (C. 13 and C. 14 contain only chapters i. ii.)

LONDON.

L. 1. = Bibl. Reg., 1. B. VIII., British Museum.
L. 2. = Bibl. Reg., 1. E. I., „ „
L. 3. = Harleian, 1793, „ „
L. 4. = Harleian, 2807, „ „
L. 5. = Harleian, 2814, „ „
L. 6. = Burney, 6, „ „
L. 7. = Sloane, 1521, „ „
L. 8. = Bibl. Reg. 1. E. VII., „ „

L. 9. = I. Sir M. Hale's MSS., Lincoln's Inn.
  (In L. 9 many leaves have been cut out; 4 Ezr. begins with ch. vi. 13.)
W. = MS. of Lat. Bible (no class-mark), in the Library of Westminster Abbey.

OXFORD.

O. 1. = Laud Lat., 12, Bodleian Library.
O. 2. = Hatton, D. 4. 8, „ „
O. 3. = Mus., D. 5. 20, „ „
O. 4. = Canon. Bibl. Lat., 67, „
O. 5. = II., New College.
O. 6. = CCCXVI., „
O. 7. = LIV., Magdalen College.

O. 8. = Canon. Bibl. Lat., 71, Bodleian Libr.
  (O. 8 contains only 4 Ezr. viii. 20—36.)

HOLKHAM.

H. = MS. of Lat. Bible in the Library of the Earl of Leicester.

DUBLIN.

Δ. = A. 1. 12, Trinity College.
(Δ. contains only 4 Ezr. viii. 20—36. I am indebted for a transcript of these verses to the Rev. Dr. B. Dickson.)

ZÜRICH.

T. = 'Cod. Turicensis,' C. 16. 5, Stadtbibliothek.
  (Collated by O. F. Fritzsche.)

DRESDEN.

D. = A. 47, Königl. öffentl. Bibliothek.
  (Collated by A. Hilgenfeld.)

non do2mı**ent ; & ap   (v. 36)
parebıt locuſ to2mentı .
30   & cum ıllo erıt locuſ re
              (fol. 62. r. *b.*)

quifitionif; & clıbanuf ge∗hen
nae oftend&² · & contra
eam ıocundıtatıf paradı
fuf & dıc& tunc altıffımↄ
ad excıtataf gentef , uıd&e   5
& ıntellegıt∗e quē negaf
tıf ✓ uel cuı non fer∗∗uıftıf ⌐
uel cuıuf dılıgentıaf fpre
uıftıf , uıd&e contra &
ın contra ⸌ hıc ıocundıtaf   10
& requıef ✓ & ıbı ıgnıf &
toↄmentɑ , haec autem
loquêrıf ⸌ dı̇cef ɑd eof; ın
dıe ıudıcıı haec talıf ✓ quı
neq; folem · neque lunā ·   15
(v. 40) neque ftellaf · neque nu
bem ⸌ neq; tonıtruum ·
neq; coↄrufcatıonem ·
neq; uentum neq; ɑquā ⸌
neque aerem nequ&e   20
nebraf ✓ neq; fero ✓ ne
que mane ⸌ neque aefta
tem · neque uɑer · ne
que ẹftūf neq; ∗hɑemē ·
ɴeq; gaelu∗ · neque frı   25
guf ⸌ neque grandınē ·
neq; pluuıam ⸌ neque
roↄē · neque merıdıem ·
neque noctem · neque
ante lucem · neq; nıtoↄē ✓   30
      (fol. 62. v. ɑ.)

neque clarıtaf · neque lux :
nıfı folūmodo fplendoↄem
clarıtatıf altıffımı ⸌ unde
omnef ıncıpıant uıdere
quẹ ante pofıta funt , fpatı
um enım habebıt fıcut ebdo
madɑ∗ ɑnnoↄum ; hoc eft
ıudıcıū meum & conftıtutı
o eıuf ✓ tᵇⁱ autē folı oftendı
haec , Et refpondı tunc &   (v. 45)
dıxı ⸌ dn̄e & nunc dıco ; beatı
∗∗∗ praefentef & obferuantef
quae autem conftıtuta f̄ ✓ fed
& quıb; hıf erat oↄatıo mea ·
quıf enım eft de prefentıb;
quı non peccauıt ✓ uel quıf
nɑtuf quı non pretẹrıbıt
fponfıonē tuɑm ⸌ Et nunc uı
deo qn̄m̄ ɑd paucof ptınebıt
futurā faeculı ıocundıtatem
facere ✓ multıf enım toↄm̄
ta , ıncreuıt enım ın nof · coↄ
malum · quod nof abẹlınaū
ab hıf ✓ & deduↄ̄ nof ın corrup
tıonem · & ⸪ itınerɑ moↄtıf; of
tendıt nobıf femₜtaf pdıtıonₑf
& longae fecıt nof ɑ uıtɑ,
& hoc non paucof fed pɑene
omnef quı creatı funt , & ref
pondıt ɑd me & dıxıt,
      (fol. 62. v. b.)

audı me & ^{ın}ſtruam te ✓ &
de ſequentı corrıpıam te ,
(v. 50) Propter hoc non ſufficit
altıſſimo unum ſaeculum
ſed duo , tu enım quıa dıxıſ   5
tı non eſſe multoſ ıuſtoſ ſed
paucoſ · ımpıoſ uero mul
tıplıcarı ✓ audı ad haec ; lapı
deſ electoſ ſi habuerıſ pau
coſ · ualde ad numerum eo2ū   10
componeſ eoſ tıbı , plum^bmum
autem & fictile habundat,
& dıxı ; dn͞e · quomodo pote
rıt ! & dıxıt ad me, non hoc
ſolum modūͦm ſed ınterro   15
ga terram & dıc& tıbı ✓ adula
(v. 55) re eı · & narrabıt tıbı · dı
cenſ ; enım & aurum creaſ^z ·
& argentum · & aeramen
tum ✓ & ferrum quoque   20
& plum^bmum · & fictıle ;
multıplı cat² autem argen
tum ſup aurum · & aera
mentum ſup argentum · &
ferrum ſup aeramentū   25
plumbū ſup ferrum ✓
& fictıle ſup plumbū ,
aeſtıma & tu ^{hec}quae ✱✱✱✱
ſint pra&ıoſa & deſide
rabılıa ✓ quod multıplıcat²   30
(fol. 63. r. a.)

aut quod rarum naſcitur ,
& dıxı ; domınato2 dn͞e · q̄d
✱abundat uılıuſ ✓ quod enım
enım rarıuſ pra&ıoſıoſ ÷ ,
& reſpondıt ad me & dıxıt
In te · ſtant · pondera quae
cogıtaſtı ✓ qn͞m qui hab&
quod dıficile ÷ ✓ gaud& ſup
eum quı hab& habundan
tıā ; ſic & amare promıſ   (v. 60)
ſa creatura , ıocunda
bo2 enım ſup paucıſ · & quı
ſaluabuntur ; propterea
quod ıpſi ſunt quı glo2ıam
meam nunc domınatıo
nem fecerunt · & per
quoſ nunc nomen meum
nomınatum eſt ; & non
conſtrıſ tabo2 ſup mul
tıtudınem eorum quı pe
rıerunt , ıpſi enım ſunt
quı ua^{pon}no nunc adſimıla
tı ſunt & flāmae ✓ ad
ſimılatae fumo adaequa
tı ſ̄ & exarſerunt ✓ ferbe
runt & extıncti ſunt, &
reſpondı & dıxı , O tu ✱ ter
ra quid peperıſti · ſi ſenſuſ
✱✱✱ factuſ ÷ de puluere
ſicut & c&era creatura ✓
(fol. 63. r. b.)

meliuſ enim erat ipſum
puluerem non eſſe natum ✓
ut non ſenſuſ inde fier& ,
nunc *autem* nobiſcum creſ
cit ſenſum . & propter hoc   5
torquemur , qnm ſcienteſ
(v. 65) perimuſ , lugeat hominum
genuſ ✓ & agreſteſ beſtiæ
la&entur ; lugeant omneſ
qui nati ſunt ✓ quadripedia   10
uero & pecora iocundæn
tur , multum enim meli
uſ eſt illiſ quam nobiſ ,
Non enim ſperant iudi
cium . nec enim ſciunt   15
cruciamenta ✓ nec ſalutē
poſt mortem repromiſ
ſam ſibi , Nobiſ *autem*
quid prod÷ qnm ſaluati
ſaluabimur . ſēd to2m   20
to to2mentabimur ✓
Omneſ enim qui nati ſunt ·
commixti ſunt iniquita
tib; ✓ & plenaé ſ peccatiſ ·
& grauati delictiſ ; & ſi   25
non eſſemuſ poſt mor
tem iudicio uenientiſ ✓
meliuſ fortaſſiſ nobiſ
(v. 70) ueniſſ& , & reſpondit
ad me , & dixit , & quan   30

(fol. 63. v. *a*.)

do *altiſſimuſ* facienſ
faciebat ſaeculum : a
dam & omneſ qui cū eo
uenerunt ✓ primū prae
parauit iudicium ✓ & quæ
ſunt iudicii , & nunc de
ſermonib; tuiſ intelle
ge ᵛ qnm dixiſti . quia
nobiſcum creſcit , qui
ergo cōmo2anteſ ſunt
in terra · hinc crucia
buntur ✓ qnm ſenſum
habenteſ · iniquitatem
fecer ✓ & mandata ac
cipienteſ . non ſeruaue
runt e*a* ✓ & legem con
ſequuti · fraudauer
eam quā acceperunt,
& quid habebunt dicere
in iudicio ✓ uel quomo
do reſpondebunt in
nouiſſimiſ tempo2ib; ✓
quātū enim tempuſ ex
quo longanimitatem
habuit * altiſſimuſ
hi*ſ qui inhabi
tant ſaeculum ✓
& non ppt eoſ ſed ppt
éa quae puidit témpo2a ;
& reſpondi ✓ & dixi ,   (v. 75)

(fol. 63. v. *b*.)

fi inueni gratiam co2ā
te dn̄e ↙ demonſtra dne
ſeruo tuo . ſi poſt mor
tem · uel nunc . quando
reddimuſ unuſ quiſ   5
que animam ſuam ↙
ſi conſeruati conſerua
bimur ᴵᴺreq̄uie , donec
ueniant tēpora illa .
in quib; incipieſ creatu   10
ram renouare ; aut amo
do cruciamur ↙ & reſ
pondit ad me & dixit ,
oſtendam tibi & hoc , tu
autem noli* commiſceri   15
cum eiſ qui ſpreuerunt ↙
neque connumereſ te
cum hiſ qui cruciantur ,
& enim ÷ tibi theſauruſ
operum repoſituſ a   20
pud altiſſimum ↙ ſed non
tibi demonſtrabitur .
uſque in nouiſſimeſ tem
po2ibuſ , Nam de mo2te
ſermoē; quando ꝓfectuſ   25
fuerit īminuſ ſenten
tiae ab altiſſimo . ut ho
mo mo2iatur · rece* *den
te inſpiratione de
co2po2e ↙ ut dimit   30
(fol. 64. r. a.)

tatur iterum ad eum qui
dedit adorare glo2iam al
tiſſimi*primum ; & ſi
quidē eſſ& eorum qui
inſpirauerunt & non ſer
uauer̄ uiam altiſſimi ·
& eo2um qui contempſer̄
legem eiuſ . & eorum qui
oderunt eoſ · qui timent eum ↙
hae* inſpirationeſ · in ha   (v. 80)
bitationeſ non ingredien
tur . ſed uaganteſ erunt
amodo in cruciamentiſ ↙
dolenteſ ſemꝑ & triſteſ ,
uia prima ↙ quia ſpreuer̄
legem altiſſimi ↙ ſaecun
da uia ↙ qn̄m non poſſunt
reuerſionē bonā facere
ut uiuant, tertia uia ↙ ui
dent repoſitam mercedem
hiſ qui teſtamtiſ altiſſi
mi crediderunt , quarta
uia ↙ conſiderabᵛant ſibi
in nouiſſimeſ repoſitum
crucia* *tuᵐᵉⁿm . quinta uia .   (v. 85)
uidenteſ alio2um habita
culū ab angeliſ conſeruari
cum ſilentio magno , ſexta
uia ↙ uidenteſ quē ad modū
de eiſ ꝑtranſienteᣞ crucia
(fol. 64. r. b.)

mentum , feptıma crucı
am̄tum uıa ✳ c̄ omnıum quę
fupra dıctae funt uıarū
maıoʒ ✓ qn̄m d&abefcent
in confufionem ✓ & confu   5
mụnt² ın horrorıb; & mar
cefcent ın tımorıbuſ ✓ uı
dentef gloʒıam altıffimı
coʒā quę̊ uıdentef pecca
uerunt ✓ & coram quo ın   10
cıpıent ın nouıffimıſ tem
porıb; ıudıcarı , Nam eo
rū quı uıaſ feruauerunt
altıffimı ✓ oʒdo ÷ hıc ; quan
do ıncıpı&ᴺ feruarı a ua   15
fo̊ coʒruptıbılı ✓ ın eo tem
poʒe cōmoʒatae · feruıe
runt cum laboʒe altıffimo ,
& omnı hoʒa fuftınuer
perıculum · ut✳ p̄fectae   20
cuftodırent legıflatoʒıſ
(v. 90) legem ✓ propter quod hıc
de hıſ fermo , ınprımıſ
uıdent cum exultatıone
multā glorıam eıuſ ✓ quı   25
fufcıpıt eaſ ; requıefcent
enım p̄ feptem ordıneſ,
Ordo prım̗ ✓ qn̄m cum la
boʒe multo certatı funt ·
ut uıncerent cum eıſ pláfına   30

(fol. 64. v. *a*.)

tum cogıtamentū malū .
ut non eaſ feducat a uı
ta, Item faecunduſ oʒdo
qn̄m uıdent complëcatı
onem ın quo uagant² ım
pıoʒū anımae ✓ & quae
ın eıſ man& punıtıo ;
tertıuſ oʒdo ✓ uıdentef teftı
monıum quoᵈ˙ teftıfıca
tuſ ÷ eıſ q̗ plafmaū̇ eaſ ✓ q̄ū̇o
uıdentef feruauer̄ quę
p̄ fidem data ÷ lex, quar   (v. 95)
tuſ ordo ✓ ıntellegenteſ re
quıem quë̊m nunc ın
promptuarııſ congrega
tı requıefcent cū fılen
tıo multo ab angelıſ con
feruatı ✓ &ᵃᵗ qu✳e ın nouıſ
fimıſ eoʒū m̈anentem glo
rıam , quıntuſ oʒdo ✓ ex
ultantef · quomodo cor
rı̈ptıbıle effugerınt nunc
& futuram quomodo
heredıtatem poffeder̄ ,
adhuc autem uıdenteſ
anguftą̈m & plenum
qn̄m lıberatı funt ✓
& fpatıofum recıpere
fruı nefcıenteſ & ınmoʒ
taleſ, fextuſ oʒdo ✓

(fol. 64. v. *b*.)

quando eif oftendit² quo
modo incipi& uultuf
eorum fulgere ficut fol ⁓
& quomodo incipient
ftellarᵘ adfimilari lumini   5
quomodo n co2rupti ,
feptimuf o2do · qui eft om
nib; fupradictif maio2 ⁓
qnm exultabunt cum fi
dutia ⁓ & qnm confident   10
bunt non confufi · & gau
debunt non reuertentef ,
feftinant enim uultum
cui feruiunt uiuentef ⁓
& a quo incipiunt glo2io   15
fi mercedem recipere ,
hic ordo animarum iuf
to2um · ut amodo anunti
entur pdictae uiae cru
ciatuf ⁓ quof patiunt² a   20
modo qui neglexerint ,
(v.100) et refpondi & dixi ,
ergo dabit² tempuf ani
mabuf poftquam fepa
rati fuerint de cor·rib;   25
ut uideant de quo mihi
dixifti ?⁓ & dixit , fep
tem dieb; erit libertaf
earum · ut uideant quæ
pdicta* f fermonef ⁓   30

(fol. 65. r. a.)

B.

& poftea congregabunt²
in habitaculif fuif, & refpon
di & dixi · fi inueni gratiam
ante oculof tuof ⁓ demonftra
mihi adhuc feruo tuo · fi in
die iudicii iufti impiof excu
fare poterint * : depcari ᵽ   : uel
eif altiffimum ; fi patref
ᵽ filiif · uel filii ᵽ parentib; ⁓ fi
fratref ᵽ fratrib; fi ad
finef ᵽ proximif ⁓ fi fiden
tef pro cariffimif · uel ᵽ fi
do* carifimuf ⁓ ut ᵽ eo
intellegat aut do2miat
aut manduc& · aut cur&* ; Et dix ;
fic nuqua nemo ᵽ aliquo ro   (v. 105)
gabit , Omnef enim po2ta
bunt · unᵽ quif que tunc in
iuftitiaf fuaf · aut iuftitiaf ,
& refpondi & dixi , & quo
modo inuenim modo qnm
roga* pm abraham ᵽᵽt
fodomitaf · & movfef

(fol. 65. r. b.)

NOTES.

fol. 62. r. *b.* l. 28   *The original reading was probably* doꝛmıbunt *as in Cod. S. Comp. a similar change in fol.* 65. *r. a. l.* 10, 11.

fol. 62. v. *a.* l. 1   ge✳hennae—c *has been erased before* h.
                  Similarly gechennam *chap.* ıı. 29.

,,   ,,   l. 2   oſtend&ꝫ—ꝫ *was originally written as an inverted comma.*

,,   ,,   l. 6   ıntellegıt✳e—a *erased.*

,,   ,,   l. 7   ſer✳✳uıſtıſ—uı *erased.*

,,   ,,   l. 18   co✳ruſcatıonem—*appar.* r *erased. Comp.* 'corruscatio' *Gloss. Lat. Bibl. Paris. antiquiss. saec.* ıx. *ed. G. F. Hildebrand, pp.* 81, 149.

,,   ,,   l. 24   ✳hảemē—c *erased.*

,,   ,,   l. 25   gaelu✳—ſ *erased.*

,,   ,,   l. 28   roꝛē—ꝛ *written over an erasure.*

fol. 62. v. *b.* l. 5   quẹ—*the* ˛ *below the* e *added in darker ink.*

,,   ,,   ,,   poſıta—ı *seems to have been added above* a *and afterwards effaced.*

,,   ,,   l. 7   ebdomada✳—*appar.* ſ *erased.*

,,   ,,   l. 9   t^{bı}—^{bı} *has been added later.*

,,   ,,   l. 12   *A word, probably* quı, *was prefixed to this line and afterwards erased.*

,,   ,,   l. 20   futurā—ā *orig.* ū.

fol. 63. r. *a.* l. 4   altıſſimo—mo *orig.* m̨.

,,   ,,   l. 11   componeſ—m *orig.* n.

,,   ,,   l. 12   *An erasure after* fictıle.

,,   ,,   l. 13   poterıt—e *written over an erasure, and* r *added at the beginning of* l. 14.

,,   ,,   l. 17   narrabıt—b *orig.* u.

fol. 63. r. *a.* l. 26, 27   plumbū—b *orig.* m.   *Du Cange gives the form 'plummum' from a Charter of the 13th century. Comp. in English 'plummet,' and the surname 'Plummer.' A like assimilation takes place in 'commurat,' 'commusta' (= comb-), and in 'ammulantibus' (= amb-). Schuchardt, Vocal. des Vulgärlateins, ı. 183, ııı. 318.*

,, ,, l. 28   haec *erased at the end of this line.*

fol. 63. r. *b.* l. 3   *abundat—*probably* h *erased.*

,, ,, ,,   quod—*orig.* quıd.

,, ,, l. 4   pra&ıofiŏſ—*the final* ſ *orig.* r.

,, ,, l. 6   *The two stops in this line written faintly by a later hand.*

,, ,, l. 11   ıocundabo2—*orig.* ıucundabo2.

,, ,, l. 19   conſtriſ tabo2—*divided thus in the MS.; for the spelling comp. 'constristatus' Mark* x. 22, *Cod. Bobbiens. (Wiener Jahrbücher der Lit. Vol.* 121.)

,, ,, l. 22   uaporı *is the result of an early correction, the last letter is retouched.*

,, ,, l. 25   ferbĕrunt—b *orig.* u.

,, ,, l. 27   *Prob.* t̄ *has been erased;* ter *is added in larger letters beyond the line.*

,, ,, l. 28, 29   *Similarly* ſuſ *has been added after the end of l.* 28, *and appar. the same syllable erased at the beginning of l.* 29.

,, ,, l. 30   c&era—c&e *written over an erasure.*

fol. 63. v. *a.* l. 7   lugeat—e *orig.* ı.

fol. 63. v. *b.* l. 18   acceperunt—*orig.* accıperunt.

,, ,, l. 23   quātū—^{n} *has been added later.*

,, ,, l. 25   habuıt—b *has been retouched,* uıt *is written over an erasure, and appar.* ÷ *erased at the end of the word.*

,, ,, l. 26   hı*ſ—ı *erased.*

fol. 64. r. *a.* l. 5   reddımuſ—ı *orig.* e, *altered by a later hand.*

,, ,, l. 8   requıe—*final* e *written over an erasure.*

,, ,, l. 15   nolı*—*appar.* ı *erased. So* nolı* *chap.* ıı. 27, vı. 10, ıx. 13, x. 34, 55. *'nolii' Matth.* ı. 20, vı. 2, 7; *John* xıı. 15, xx. 27, *Book of Deer (ed. for the Spalding Club by* J. Stuart, 1869). *Luke* vııı. 49, 50,

Rushworth Gospels (ed. Skeat). *Comp.* audı∗ *chap.* VII. 2, VIII. 19, XI. 16, *and 'oboediite' Hebr.* XIII. 17, *Cod. Clarom.* (*ed. Tischend.*)

fol. 64. r. *a*. l. 17   connumeref—*orig.* connumerıf.

 ,, ,, l. 21   apud—*orig.* aput.

 ,, ,, l. 28   rece∗ ∗den—*the second* e *is due to an old corrector, and* den *is added beyond the line.*

fol. 64. r. *b*. l. 3   *A stop erased before* prımum.

 ., ,, l. 4   quıdc̄—e *has been retouched.*

 ,, ,, l. 10   hae∗—e *written over an erasure;* appar. c *erased after it, as also in chap.* XIII. 40.

 ,, ,, ,,   ınfpıratıonef—e *orig.* ı.

 ,, ,, l. 29   uıa—a *orig.* a.

fol. 64. v. *a*, l. 2   *Appar.* ÷ *erased, and* c̄ *substituted.*

 ,, ,, ,,   quẹ *added later beyond the line.*

 ,, ,, l. 6   horrorıb;—*orig.* honorıb;. *Comp. Ecclus.* I. 14, *where Cod. Amiat. has* '*horribilis*' *and ed. Sixtino-Clem.* '*honorabilis;*' *and Mal.* I. 14, *where the former has* '*honorabile*' *and the latter* '*horribile.*' (*See Bibl. S. Lat. V. T. ed. Heyse et Tischendorf.*)

 ,, ,, l. 10   quo—uo *written over an erasure.*

 ,, ,, l. 19   fuftınueī—ı *orig.* e (*corr. by later hand*).

 ., ,, l. 20   ut∗—*appar. final* ı *erased.*

fol. 64. v. *b*. l. 10   plafmaū—*orig.* plafmaū, ᶦᵗ *added in lighter ink.*

 ,, ,, l. 15   promptuarıf—o *orig.* u.

 ,, ,, l. 18   qu∗e—a *partially erased.*

 ,, ,, l. 22   corrꞇ́ptıbıle—e *orig.* ı.

 ., ,, l. 23   futuram—a *orig.* u.

fol. 65. r. *a*. l. 5   ftellarᵘ—*there is a trace of a mark of abbreviation above* r.

 ,, ., l. 10   fidutıa—t *orig.* c.—NT (*written in a compound form*) *added at the end of the line.*

 ,, ,, l. 11   confufı—*there is a slight trace of* f *written above* u.

 ,, ,, l. 20   quof—o *seems to have been orig.* a.

fol. 65. r. *a*. l. 30   p̄dıctȧ*—*prob.* e *erased.*

fol. 65. r. *b*. l. 7   *Prob. & erased in this line*—uel *substituted in the margin.*

,, ,, l. 9   uel *written over an erasure.*

,, ,, l. 11   a͛dfineſ—e *orig.* ı.

,, ,, l. 12   uel *written over an erasure.*

,, ,, ,,   ⲣ fí—*added beyond the line.*

fol. 65. r. *b*. l. 13   do*—o *orig.* u—*final* ſ *erased.*

,, ,, ,,   carıſimuſ—*final* ſ *written over an erasure*—m *erased.*

,, ,, l. 15   cur&*—*orig.* cur&²—Et dıx̄ ; *added at the end of the line.*

,, ,, l. 17   rogabıt—b *orig.* u.

,, ,, l. 21   ınuenı͛mus—uen *written over an erasure.*

,, ,, l. 22   roga*—*orig.* rogaū, ᵘⁱᵗ *added in lighter ink.*

4 EZRA VII. 36—105.

36 ET apparebit lacus tormenti, et contra illum erit locus requietionis; et clibanus
37 gehennae ostendetur, et contra eum iocunditatis paradisus. Et dicet tunc Altissimus ad excitatas gentes : uidete et intellegite quem negastis, uel cui non

(In the notes immediately below the text both the original readings and the later corrections found in the MS. are printed in Italics).

36. lacus *locus.* contra illum *cum illo.* requietionis *requisitionis.* eum *eam*

36. If we possessed only the Lat. vers., the *locus tormenti* of our MS. might pass unchallenged (comp. Luke xvi. 28, Cod. Bezae Lat.); but there can be no doubt that *locus* is an echo from the following clause, (as the second *uenae* is from the preceding clause in chap. iv. 7, where the MSS. have *uenae...uenae* for *uenae...uiae*), and that, with the authority of the other versions, we must read *lacus tormenti.* With this comp. *cum deducerent eum ad infernum cum his qui descendunt in lacum,* Ezek. xxxi. 16 Hieron. Vet. Lat. (a chap. from which other reminiscences may be traced in 4 Ezra), and *de lacu miseriae,* Ps. xxxix. 3 (so conversely in Rev. xviii. 17, *qui in locum nauigat,* Codd. Amiat. et Fuld., has been corrupted into *qui in lacum nau.,* ed. Sixtino-Clement.). This phrase is rendered ὁ κόλπος τῶν βασάνων in Hilgenfeld's attempted restoration of the Greek : but ὁ κόλπος is derived solely from the Syr. ܟܘܒܐ, which is scarcely satisfactory ; for this I propose to read ܓܘܒܐ 'puteus', 'fouea' = جُبّ of the Arab. Compendium (Arab.²). For another instance of the confusion of the letters ܒ and ܠ in the MS., see chap. xi. 37, Ceriani's note. By these

two slight emendations, the Lat., Syr., Æth., and Arab. versions are brought into harmony with one another, and all point to an original ὁ λάκκος τῆς βασάνου.

et contra illum erit locus requietionis] The Syr. and Æth. verss. suggest this emendation ; *requietionis* was probably first corrupted into *requisitionis,* and the introduction of this new word involved the further change of *contra illum* to *cum illo.* In the Arab. vers. نِيَاح (not نِيَاخ) = Syr. ܢܝܚܐ. See Fleischer, *Zeitschr. d. D. M. G.,* vol. XVIII. p. 291, and Com. de Baudissin, *Transl. Ant. Arab. Libri Iobi quae supers.* p. 111.

iocund. parad.]= ὁ τῆς τρυφῆς παράδεισος. Comp. the LXX in Gen. ii. 15 (Cod. Vat.), iii. 23, 24; Ezek. xxxi. 9, Joel ii. 3; the pl. τῶν τρυφῶν in Hilgenf. rests only on the ribbui of the Syr.

37. For Hilgenfeld's Gk. καὶ ἐρεῖ τότε ὁ ὕψιστος κατὰ τῶν λαῶν τῶν ἐξεγερθέντων I would substitute κ. ἐ. τ. ὁ ὕψ. πρὸς τὰ ἔθνη τὰ ἐξεγερθέντα, which best explains all the versions, not excepting the Syr., for πρὸς may be well rendered by ܠܘܩܒܠ in such a context, comp. Luke xviii. 9 Pesh.

38 seruiuistis, uel cuius diligentias spreuistis. Uidete contra et in contra: hic iocun-
ditas et requies, et ibi ignis et tormenta; haec autem loqueris dicens ad eos in
39 die iudicii. Hic talis qui neque solem [habeat] neque lunam, neque stellas,

38, 39. dicens ad eos in die iudicii; Hic talis...dice^ns ad eos; in die iudicii h̩a̩e̩c talis...
39. solem [habeat] *solem.*

For *populis resuscitatorum*, in Hilgenfeld's emended translation of the Arab., read *populis qui resuscitati sunt* (according to Ockley's construction), which is the correct rendering of the vulg. Arab. للَّابِم الذين قاموا, and agrees with the other versions.

The word *diligentiam*, which occurs in chap. iii. 19 in parallelism with *legem*, has been a source of much perplexity to commentators; we have here another instance of the same peculiar use of this word. It naturally came to mean scrupulous attention to commands, and particularly to religious duties. Comp. *diligentia mandatorum tuorum*, Cic.; *sacrorum diligentia*, id.; *tanquam diligentiam suam etiam ipsi Deo praeferentibus*, Iren. iv. 11, Old Lat. trans.: just as, on the other hand, *indiligentia* is used for neglect of duty, or trespass, in the old Lat. vers. of Leviticus, ed. by Lord Ashburnham (1869): e.g. in chap. v. 16, 18, vi. 6, where the Gk. is πλημμέλεια; similarly chap. v. 19, *Insuper enim habebit indiligentiam* (not *quaecunque deliquerit*, as quoted by Ranke, *Par Palimps. Wirceburg.* p. 231) *indiligens fuit ante Deum*, where the Gk. is ἐπλημμέλησε γὰρ πλημμελεία ἔναντι κυρίου. Comp. also v. 15. In other passages of this vers. πλημμελεῖν and πλημμέλεια are represented by *negligere* and *negligentia*. In these instances the Greek word doubtless suggested this translation, in accordance with the etymology which we find set forth at length by one who fondly clung to the Old Lat. vers. *Et πλημμέλεια simile nomen est negligentiae: nam Graece negligentia ἀμέλεια dicitur, quia curae non est quod negligitur. Sic enim Graecus dicit, Non curo, οὐ μέλει μοι. Particula ergo quae additur πλήν, ut dicatur πλημμέλεια, praeter significat, ut ἀμέλεια quod uocatur negligentia, uideatur sonare sine cura, πλημμέλεια praeter curam, quod pene tantundem est. Hinc et quidam nostri πλημμέλειαν non delictum, sed negligentiam interpretari maluerunt. In latina autem lingua quid aliud negligitur nisi quod non legitur, id est non eligitur? Unde etiam legem a legendo, id est ab eligendo latini auctores appellatum esse dixerunt.* August. quaest. in Levit. § xx. The word *diligentia*, as used in the 4th book of Ezra, by a natural transition takes the meaning of that which is to be observed,—an observance; just as מִשְׁמֶרֶת by a similar process becomes associated with laws and ordinances. Gen. xxvi. 5; Deut. xi. 1. Comp. also *obseruationes*, Lev. xviii. 30 (Ashb.). In a paper read by me before the Cambridge Hebr. Soc. in 1869 I pointed out that *diligere uiam tuam*, ch. iii. 7 (Syr. = mandatum, Æth. = mandatum iustitiae), must stand in close connexion with *diligentiam*, iii. 19 (Syr. = mandata. Æth. = mandatum). I now find my conjecture confirmed by Codd. A. and S., both of which have in the former place *diligentiam unam tuam.* See p. 28.

38, 39. The Syr. and Æth. verss. suggest the following reading: *haec loquetur ad eos in die iudicii, dies enim iudicii talis qui ....*

39. *neque solem...*] The Arab. alone inserts an additional noun here: *In illo die non erit neque sol, neque lux, neque luna, neque stella, neque nubes...* (*lucem dans* appended to *sol* in the Arm. seems from the context to be a mere expletive). We find the same sequence in Eccles. xii. 2 *antequam tenebrescat sol, et lumen, et luna, et stellae, et reuertantur nubes...*

[*habeat*] The insertion of some such verb is required by the structure of the sentence, and introduces less disturbance than the substitution of *cui* for *qui* and of the nom. for the accus. in the following nouns. Of the nine MSS. of the Æth. vers. in the Brit. Mus. one only (Or. 490) has the reading *albāti d̩ahaya* 'non habet (dies iud.) solem.' The reading of the others *albō dahay* 'non est sol' favours the conjectural emendation of Van der Vlis, yet they do not all (see especially Or. 489) consistently maintain the nom. case throughout the series.

40 Neque nubem, neque tonitruum, neque coruscationem, neque uentum, neque aquam,
41 neque aerem, neque tenebras, neque sero, neque mane, Neque aestatem, neque
uer, neque aestum, neque hiemem, neque gelu, neque frigus, neque grandi-
42 nem, neque pluuiam, neque rorem, Neque meridiem, neque noctem, neque ante
lucem, neque nitorem, neque claritatem, neque lucem, nisi solummodo splendorem

41. aestum *çstus* altered to *estū*. gelu *gaelus* altered to *gelu*.
42. claritatem *claritas* altered to *claritatem*. neque lucem *neque lux* altered to *neque lucem*.

40. *neque tonitr., neque corusc.*] This is also the order in Ambrose (see extract A.). In the Syr. and Æth. verss. it is inverted.

sero] This form is probably due to the predominant adverbial use of such words; *serum* might be thought to range better with the nouns in the list, but though we have such phrases as *quia serum erat diei*, Liv. VII. 8, *in serum dimicatione protracta*, Suet. Aug. 17, and *serum* as an occasional variant for *sero* in the formula *sero factum est*, e.g. in Judith xiii. 1, Cod. Pech. (Sab.), Mark iv. 35, Cod. Pal. (ed. Tischend.), comp. Mark xi. 19, xiv. 17, Cod. Bobbiens. (ed. Tisch., *Wiener Jahrbücher der Lit.* Vols. 121, 123), yet it would be difficult to find in the Latin of this period examples of *serum* used absolutely like its modern derivatives 'sera,' 'soir,' as an equivalent for *vesper*, the word which Ambrose substitutes in his paraphrase of this passage. Isidore of Sevilla (Sacc. VII.) seems to bring us nearer to this use of the word, in the curious etymology which he proposes: *serum uocatum a clausis seris, quando nox uenit, ut unusquisque somno tutior sit*. Orig. Lib. v. 30, 17.

41. In attempting to explain the variations of the different versions in this long enumeration, we must make some allowance for the idiom of language, which groups words together according to a natural affinity. The two seasons which come first in order are thus represented by the three leading authorities: Lat. *aestas, uer*; Syr. *aestas, hiems*; Æth. *hiems, aestas*. Now, referring to Zach. xiv. 8 and Ps. lxxiii. 17 קַיִץ וָחֹרֶף, LXX. θέρος καὶ ἔαρ, we find in the Old Lat. (Sab.), the Syr. (Pesh.), and the Æth. respectively, the same two seasons linked together as in the corresponding translations of this verse.

Again, the Syr. and Æth. verss. have three seasons, the Lat. two only, unless we suppose *hiemem*

B.

to be displaced. Comp. the paraphrase of Ambrose, *neque aestas neque hiems uices uariabunt temporum*, but this cannot be pressed. The present position of *hiemem* after *aestum* is probably due to its second signification 'storm' (χειμών). In some copies of the Æth. there is a similar combination, since after *aestum* (for which *sudor* is unfortunately given both in Laurence and Hilgenf.) follows *procella* according to the Berlin MS. (Prætorius) and the majority of the MSS. in the Brit. Mus. Similarly in the Arab. a word for 'storm' comes immediately after the seasons. For *aestus* (before *autumnus*) in the Lat. transl. from the Arab. we must read *aestas*.

Ewald explains لنافس as the pl. fract. of لنفس = λαμπάς. I may notice, however, that this word has been altered in the MS.; the base of the ا has been apparently retouched, the ن was originally ا, and ن has been erased before ف. The *lucerna* of Hilgenf. can scarcely be accepted as an adequate translation of the term; it would rather, I conceive, be illustrated by the λαμπάδες of Exod. xx. 18. But in the absence of any other example, the existence of such a word in Arab. must be regarded as doubtful.

42. *ante lucem*] The other verss. lead us to expect a noun here as above in v. 40, and it is not improbable that in the original text of the Lat. there stood the rare word *antelucium*. We have a trace of this form as a var. for *anteluculo*, Apul. *Met.* I. 14 (ed. Hildebr.); and examples of the ablative are found in Apul. *Met.* I. 11, and IX. 15. It is worth noticing in connexion with the reading of our MS. that in both these passages we find as a var. for *antelucio* the easier expression *ante lucem*. In

8

43 claritatis Altissimi, unde omnes incipiant uidere quae anteposita sunt. Spatium
44 enim habebit sicut ebdomada annorum. Hoc est iudicium meum et constitutio eius,
45 tibi autem soli ostendi haec. Et respondi tunc et dixi: domine, et nunc dico:
46 beati praesentes et obseruantes quae a te constituta sunt; Sed et [de] quibus
   erat oratio mea, quis enim est de praesentibus, qui non peccauit, uel quis natus,
47 qui non praeteriuit sponsionem tuam? Et nunc uideo, quoniam ad paucos per-
48 tinebit futuram saeculi iocunditatem facere, multis autem tormenta. Increuit enim

43. ebdomada *ebdomada*∗.
45. a te *autem* altered to *a te;* so also in chap. xiv. 21.
46. Sed et [de] quibus erat...praeteriuit *sed et quib; his erat... præteribit.*
47. futuram *futurū* altered to *futurā.* autem *enim.*

Ecclus. xxiv. 44 we have *antelucanum* as a rendering of ὄρθρον.

43, 44. *harum rerum* (16), and *horum omnium*
(17), should change places in the Lat. transl. from
the Arab. (Hilgenf. p. 341).

44. *et constitutio eius*] Comp. *haec est constitutio legis,* Num. xix. 2, Cod. Ashburnh. In the Syr.
ܗܢܘ ܕܝܢ ܘܢܡܘܣܗ *hoc est autem et lex eius,*
Cer., for ܕܝܢ *autem,* read ܕܝܠܝ *iudicium meum.*

45. The Syr. suggests the transposition of the
words *tunc et,* and is besides more flowing: *Et respondi et dixi: Dominator Domine, etiam tunc
dixi, et nunc iterum dicam;* while in chap. ix. 15,
olim locutus sum is not represented in the Syr.

praesentes et obs. gives the sense of the Arab.
rather than Ockley's explan., *that are found keeping.*

46. *Sed et [de] quibus erat oratio mea*] It is difficult to decide between the various possible com-
binations of the Lat. words in our MS., but *de quibus* (or *de his*) seems to be the simplest emendation.
Ewald's restoration: *Doch meine frage an dich ist
die,* is based on the Æth.; while the Lat., the Arab.
and also the Syr. (comp. ܒܥܬܐ vii. 102, 106
(36)), require the noun in the Gk. to be δέησις rather
than ἐρώτησις. Perhaps an orig. of the form: ἀλλὰ
καὶ περὶ ὧν (or περὶ τούτων) ἡ δέησίς μου would best
account for this divergence in translation, together
with the difference in tense. The same sentiment
reappears in chap. viii. 17. Comp. Rom. x. 1.

47. *quoniam ad paucos pertinebit*] From the
Syr. vers. we may restore the original Greek thus:

ὅτι ὀλίγοις μὲν μελλήσει ὁ αἰὼν ὁ ἐρχόμενος εὐφροσύνην
ποιεῖν, πολλοῖς δὲ βασάνους. It is evident that the
Latin translator read μελλήσει *pertinebit,* for μελλήσει
incipiet; the effects of this error extend to the end
of the sentence. I have altered *enim* to *autem;*
these particles are frequently interchanged in MSS.,
e.g. in chap. vii. 18 our MS. has *autem,* Cod. S. *enim.*

48. *Increuit enim in nos cor malum*] For this
accus. after *in* comp. *et in pectus meum increscebat
sapientia,* chap. xiv. 40, Cod. S. and Rönsch, p. 410.

et in itinera mortis] Instead of *in,* which is
added above the line, the Syr. supplies *monstrauit
nobis;* the Æth., however, has coupled this with the
following clause, thus: *et deduxit nos in uiam mortis
et in uiam perditionis.*

et hoc non paucos, sed pene omnes qui creati sunt]
The Syr. has: ܘܗܢܐ ܠܐ ܗܘܐ ܠܩܠܝܠܐ
ܐܠܐ ܢܕܪ ܕܟܠܗܘܢ ܐܝܠܝܢ ܕܐܬܒܪܝܘ
where the word ܢܕܪ has occasioned much embar-
rassment. Ceriani originally regarded it as corrupted from ܟܒܪ 'fortassis;' he afterwards was
inclined to retain the MS. reading with the rendering 'simul,' 'coniunctim,' though the difficulties of
construction did not escape him. In the Lat. now
published, we first meet with a corresponding particle, *pene;* this might seem rather to favour the
emendation proposed by Ceriani, but there would
still be an objection to the ܕ following ܢܕܪ, so
that we are driven to reconsider the ܢܕܪ of the
MS. Now this reading (if we disregard the upper

in nos cor malum, quod nos abalienauit ab his, et deduxit nos in corruptionem, et
in itinera mortis, ostendit nobis semitas perditionis et longe fecit nos a uita; et hoc
49 non paucos, sed pene omnes qui creati sunt. Et respondit ad me et dixit: audi
50 me et instruam te, et de sequenti corripiam te: Propter hoc non fecit Altissimus
51 unum saeculum, sed duo. Tu enim, quia dixisti non esse multos iustos, sed paucos,
52 impios uero multiplicari, audi ad haec: Lapides electos si habueris paucos ualde,

48. et in itinera & *in*itinera.
49. instruam *in*struam.
50. non fecit Altissimus *non sufficit altissimus* -mus altered to -mo.
52. paucos ualde, ad num. *paucos, ualde ad num.*

point) is strongly supported by a similar construction in the Syr. of Ecclus. xxx. 4, which has hitherto been obscured by a mistranslation. The verse stands thus in the Gk. and Syr. versions from the lost Hebr.: ἐτελεύτησεν αὐτοῦ ὁ πατήρ, καὶ ὡς οὐκ (καὶ οὐχ ὡς א. καὶ οὐκ ὡς A.) ἀπέθανεν (ܐܚܘ ܐܪܟܐ ܕܠܐ ܟܝܒ Syr. Hex. ed. Cer.) ὅμοιον γὰρ αὐτῷ κατέλιπε μετ’ αὐτόν.—ܘܐܟܒܪܝ ܐܟܐܣܡ ܕܝܒ ܕܠܐ ܟܝܒ. ܕܠܐ ܡܛܠ ܘܐܟܘܬܗ ܒܥܩ ܒܬܪܗ. The Syr. is thus interpreted in the Par. and Lond. Polyglots: 'Defuncto ipsius patre, *superest* alter haud mortuus; quandoquidem similem sui post se reliquit.' The ܘܟܒܪܝ here (for so we are directed to write the word, in the recension of the text by Jacob of Edessa, Brit. Mus., MS. Rich. 7183 fol. 81 b. 1, l. 11) is evidently inaccurately represented by '*superest* alter,' and the true sense of the clause might be correctly expressed in the words of the Old Lat.: *et quasi non est mortuus*. In fact ܟܒܪܝ (or ܟܒܪܝ ܕ. when a noun does not immediately succeed) = 'companion of,' 'allied to,' seems to pass into the meaning of 'well nigh,' 'as if,' 'one might almost say.' The use of חָבֵר in Prov. xxviii. 24 may be looked on as the germ of this formula. As, however, in the absence of other examples, the existence of such a particle must still be considered doubtful, I leave these few hints to be confirmed, or otherwise, by subsequent research.

49. *instruam*] For the earlier reading *struam* comp. *de quibus structus es*, Luke i. 4, Cod. Bezae, and the reff. to Tert. in Rönsch, p. 380; also *ad in*struendos (var. *struendos*) *istinc nos*, Cypr. Epist. XLIV. 1 (ed. Hartel). In chap. v. 32, where the same phrase occurs, *instruam* is without a variant.

et de sequenti corripiam te] Prob. from the Gk. καὶ ἐκ δευτέρου νουθετήσω σε. For de sequenti (Syr. ܒܝܪܬܝܢܘ), comp. denuo, de integro, de futuro, de praeterito, &c. *Sequens = secundus* vi. 7, 9, xi. 13.

50. *non fecit Altissimus*] I have ventured to substitute these words for the present reading of our MS., *non sufficit Altissimo*; for a recurrence to the original *Altissimus* involves a change of the verb (comp. *hoc saeculum fecit Altissimus*, chap. viii. 1), and by this emendation the Lat. is brought into conformity with all the other versions.

51. *impios uero multiplicari*] This clause is represented in the Arab., Arab.[2] (Cod. Vat.), and Arm., but not in the Syr. There is a lacuna in the Æth.

52. *ad numerum eorum...abundat*] The Lat. has been here interpolated; it should rather run thus: *ad numerum eorum compones tibi plumbum et fictile*. The words *eos, autem* and *abundat* distort the argument and find no place in any other version. The comparison implies that the number of the elect (to borrow the epithet used in the Lat.) cannot be increased by the addition of baser elements; this sense is best expressed by the Arab. The pron. *eorum* is not absent from any of the versions, although omitted in the Lat. translations of the Æth. and Arab. In the Æth. the latter part of v. 51 and the beginning of v. 52 have fallen out through homœotel. The problem of making a leaden vessel out of clay is a difficulty merely introduced in Laurence's transl.; the correct rendering, *make for thyself a vessel of lead and clay*, reflects the same original as

53 ad numerum eorum compones eos tibi, plumbum autem et fictile abundat. Et
54 dixi: domine, quomodo poterit? Et dixit ad me: non hoc solummodo, sed interroga
55 terram, et dicet tibi, adulare ei, et narrabit tibi, Dices ei: aurum creas et
56 argentum et aeramentum, et ferrum quoque et plumbum et fictile; Multiplicatur
   autem argentum super aurum, et aeramentum super argentum, et ferrum super
57 aeramentum, plumbum super ferrum, et fictile super plumbum. Aestima et tu,
   quae sint pretiosa et desiderabilia, quod multiplicatur aut quod rarum nascitur.
58 Et dixi: dominator domine, quod abundat uilius, quod enim rarius pretiosius est.
59. Et respondit ad me et dixit: In te †stant pondera quae cogitasti, quoniam qui habet
60 quod difficile est, gaudet super eum, qui habet abundantiam; Sic et a me repromissa

54. solummodo solummodo*u̇m*.   55. Dices ei: aurum creas *dicens*; *enim & aurum* crea*s*
57. quae *quae haec* altered to *haec quae*.
58. enim *enim enim*. pretiosius *praetiosior* altered to *pretiosius*.
60. Sic et a me repromissa creatura *sic & amare promissa creatura*.

the other versions, but the verb συνθήσεις, taken in the meaning of 'construct,' required the insertion of an object before the materials.

54. *adulare* seems to import a needless intensity into a simple appeal; no stronger word than *loquere* is required by the other versions.

55. Comp. chap. viii. 2. By substituting *dices* for *dicens*, and *ei* for *et*, I have brought this Latin clause into harmony with the other versions. A strong argument that it originally followed the same construction may be derived from the reading *creas* (pr. m.), for the 2nd pers. sing. of a similar verb is found in all the other verss. In the sentence, as read by the principal translators, it looks as if the substance of the earth's reply were anticipated by the interrogator. The corrector of our MS. recognized this difficulty, and attempted to elicit an intelligible sense by reading: *dicens; et aurum creatur...* The answer would begin at *multiplicatur* according to Ewald: *so wird sie dir erwidern, aber des silbers ist mehr als gold...* In the Arm. also and Arab. a new speaker is here introduced.

59. There is a startling error in the MS. reading of this passage: *in te stant pondera*. An explanation that readily occurs is, that *stant* is a corruption from *statera* (in Ecclus. xxi. 25 ἐν ζυγῷ σταθήσονται = *statera ponderabuntur*). It may be urged that the noun is here superfluous and not expressed in the other versions, but this difficulty will be removed

by supposing the original to have been, as Mr. Hort suggests, ζυγοστάτησον, which might be rendered either by one word or by two, and which is used in this metaphorical sense by Lucian, *De Hist. Conscrib.* c. 49: καὶ ζυγοστατείτω τότε ὥσπερ ἐν τρυτάνῃ τὰ γιγνόμενα; and by Eulog. ap. Phot. *Bibl.* p. 272. 35 (ed. Bekker): τὰ δὲ ῥήματα τῇ διανοίᾳ ζυγοστατεῖν.

It may be worth while to mention another attempt to account for the presence of *stant*. In the Syr. the clause stands thus: ܕܐܝܬ ܣܡ ܡܘܬ ܒܝܢܬܟ. The same phrase is found in chap. iv. 31, where the Lat. is: *aestima autem* (=δή, ˙Hilgenf.) *apud te*. Now the Tironian sign for *autem*, ⱶ, which was probably not very familiar to our scribe (I have noted only two instances of it in this book), might have been here read as ſt. Whichever be the solution, it is clear that the termination *-ant* originated from a copyist (possibly influenced by chap. xiv. 14) mistaking the imperat. *pondera* for a plur. noun.

The corresponding clause in Ewald's 'Wiederherstellung des Buches,' *es ziemt dir wohl so zu denken*, seems to have been derived solely from Laurence's transl. of the Æth. *Te ipso id dignum sit, quod cogitasti* (retained in Hilgenf.). This version, however, if correctly rendered, would conform to the Syr., and to the orig. Lat. vers. See Dillm. *Lex.* s. voc. I. 6.

60. *Sic et a me repromissa creatura*] I have

creatura, iocundabor enim super paucis et qui saluabuntur, propterea quod ipsi sunt
qui gloriam meam nunc dominatiorem fecerunt, et per quos nunc nomen meum

61 nominatum est; Et non contristabor super multitudinem eorum qui perierunt, ipsi
enim sunt qui uapori assimilati sunt et flammae, fumo adaequati sunt et exarserunt,

62 feruerunt et extincti sunt. Et respondi et dixi: O tu terra, quid peperisti, si sensus

63 factus est de puluere, sicut et cetera creatura! Melius enim erat ipsum puluerem

64 non esse natum, ut non sensus inde fieret. Nunc autem nobiscum crescit sensus,

65 et propter hoc torquemur, quoniam scientes perimus. Lugeat hominum genus, et

60. dominatiorem *dominationem.*
61. uapori apparently *uano* altered to *uapori.* fumo *adsimilatae fumo.*
feruerunt *feruerunt* altered to *ferbuerunt.*
64. sensus *sensum* altered to *sensus.*

thus attempted to emend the *sic et amare promissa creatura* of our MS., but the sense is still unsatisfactory, and a comparison with the other versions shews that this is another instance of the confusion between κτίσις and κρίσις in the Greek of our book. Comp. Hilgenf. pp. XL. XLI. A still earlier form of the Lat., to judge from the Syr. and Æth., was *repromissio creaturae,* the original being probably οὕτως καὶ ἡ παρ' ἐμοῦ ἐπαγγελία τῆς κρίσεως (var. lect. κτίσεως).

qui gloriam meam nunc dominatiorem fecerunt] The Syr. and Arab.² = *qui nunc gloriam meam confirmant.* The Æth. = *quoniam illi assequentur gloriam meam.* The Gk. οἱ...κυροῦντες would explain both these renderings, but the verb κυρεῖν seems too remote from the Gk. vocabulary of the Æth. translator. It might be urged in favour of the retention of the MS. reading *dominationem,* that the phrase in the original was possibly κυρίαν ποιεῖν, and that our translator took the former word for κυρείαν; but the construction of the clause requires us, I think, by the change of a single letter, to read *dominatiorem,* a word used as equivalent to κυριώτερος in the old Lat. translation of Irenaeus, e.g., II. 5. 4 (ed. Stieren), *alioquin necessitatem maiorem et dominatiorem facient quam Deum.* The corruption in the MS. is well illustrated by a passage in Tert. *adv. Marc.* I. XXVIII. (ed. Oehler): *Credo, sulphuratiorem eis gehennam praeparabit,* where the analogous form *sulphuratiorem* has for a

variant the abstract *sulphurationem.* And so also *timoratior,* which is Volkmar's acute emendation for the common reading *timor acrior* in 4 Ezra xii. 13, appears in our MS. as *timoratio.*

61. The Arab. has صاروا مستوجبين للنار 'have proved worthy of,' 'are condemned to the fire;' Ockley, *are bound to hell.* Fabricius, unskilled in Engl. idiom (by an obvious association he translates *craftiness* by *vires* in verse 92), has rendered this *ligati ad infernum* (retained in Hilgenf.).

62. *O tu terra, quid peperisti*] The Syr. gives this in an expanded form: *O quid fecisti, terra, quia isti nati sunt e te et ambulant in perditionem,* comp. chap. x. 10. The Arm. sums up this and the two following verses in a similar expression: *O terra, quare genuisti hominem? nam cruciatibus aeternitatis traditus est.*

63. In this verse the Latin gives no countenance to Le Hir's interpretation of the Syr. (see *Monum. sacra et prof.* ed. Ceriani, vol. v. p. 110); the word ܕܝܢ however, to which he gives the inadmissible translation *iudicium,* is certainly out of place; omitting this, and a superfluous ܕ in ܐܬܪܠܐ, we might restore the original thus: κρεῖσσον γὰρ (−γὰρ Syr.) ἦν εἰ οὐκ ἐγεννήθη (+καὶ Syr.) αὐτὸς ὁ χοῦς ἵνα μὴ γένηται ὁ νοῦς ἐκεῖθεν. But we cannot expect perfect conformity between the Lat. and the Syr., as the addition of an extra clause to verse 62 in the latter has disturbed the balance of the sentence.

agrestes bestiae laetentur, lugeant omnes qui nati sunt, quadripedia uero et pecora
66 iocundentur. Multum enim melius est illis quam nobis, non enim sperant iudicium,
67 nec enim sciunt cruciamenta nec salutem post mortem repromissam sibi. Nobis autem
68 quid prodest, quoniam saluati saluabimur, si tormento tormentabimur? Omnes enim
qui nati sunt, commixti sunt iniquitatibus, et pleni sunt peccatis, et grauati delictis;
69 Et si non essemus post mortem in iudicio uenientes, melius fortassis nobis uenisset.
70 Et respondit ad me et dixit: et quando Altissimus faciens faciebat saeculum, Adam
et omnes qui cum eo uenerunt, primum praeparauit iudicium et quae sunt iudicii.
71 Et nunc de sermonibus tuis intellege, quoniam dixisti, quia nobiscum crescit sensus;

65. omnes *omnes* altered to *homines*.
67. quoniam *qnm* altered to *quod*. si *sed* altered to *si*.
69. in iudicio uenientes *in iudicio uenientis*.
71. intellege...crescit sensus; Qui *intellege* *vel sensum*, ...*crescit, qui*...

66. *Multum enim melius*] In like manner our
MS. has *multum* (for *multo*) *plus uae his*, chap. xiii.
16. This use of 'multum' with a comparative, not
unknown in classical authors, as Plaut. *Most*. iii. 2.
137, Cic. *Off*. iii. 13 (55) (in some MSS.), Stat. *Theb*.
ix. 559, Sil. Ital. xiii. 708, Juv. x. 197, Quintil. *Instit*.
x. 1. 94, is of rare occurrence in biblical MSS. According to Vercellone, some authorities have *multum*
as a variant in Ruth iv. 15, *et multo tibi melior est*.
The same construction in Gk. is more familiar from
Homer downwards; comp. also 4 Macc. i. 8, ii. 6,
2 Cor. viii. 22, 1 Pet. i. 7 (text. rec.), and πολὺ (text.
rec., πολλῷ) μᾶλλον Heb. xii. 9, 25. This should not
be confounded with πολὺ μᾶλλον ἢ in Num. xiv. 12,
Deut. ix. 14, which is an attempt to represent the
Hebr. idiom for the comparative of the adj. See
Is. liv. 1, LXX.

In Arab.² we must read with the MS.

.(اكراثهم) لقلة اكتراثهم (not

The other versions have no particle corresponding to the third *enim* in this verse.

68. *commixti sunt iniquitatibus*] Perhaps συμ-
πεφυρμένοι εἰσὶν ἀνομίαις; at least there is a strong
probability that some form of φύρεσθαι stood in the
original of this clause, for the ܚܒܝܟܝܢ of the
Syr. (comp. the Syro-Hex. of Is. xiv. 19, Lam. iv. 14
Sym., Ezek. xvi. 6, 22, Job vii. 5, xxx. 14, xxxix. 30,
Jer. iii. 2), and the مجونين (=πεφυραμένοι) of
the Arab., both point in this direction. The Gk.

word in this context may be illustrated by συμφυρό-
μενον ἐν ταῖς ἁμαρτίαις αὐτοῦ, Ecclus. xii. 14; συμ-
φυρμοὺς πονηρίας, Herm. *Past*. Vis. ii. 2; καὶ ταῖς
πραγματείαις σου συνανεφύρης ταῖς πονηραῖς, id. Vis.
ii. 3; and συμφύρεσθαι τῷ τῆς πονηρίας αὐτῶν βορ-
βόρῳ, Eus. *Hist. Eccles*. vii. 7. 2. For the Syr.
comp. ܐܠܡܝܢ ܕܚܛܝܢܝܢ ܒܚܛܗܝܟܘܢ
ܒܒܝܫܬܐ, Apocal. Bar. 21.

grauati delictis] In the transl. from the Syr.
vers. ܡܦܘܠܬܐ (pl. of ܡܦܘܠܬܐ, chap. iii. 1,
see Amira, *Gram. Syr*. p. 92) should not be rendered *ruinae*, which is its proper meaning in Apocal.
Bar. 35, but *delicta*, both here and in chap. vii. 23.
The Syr. word is equivalent not only to πτῶσις, Is.
xvii. 1, li. 17 (Hex.), and to πτῶμα, Job xv. 23, xvi. 14
(Hex.), but also to παράπτωμα, Job xxxv. 15 (Hex.),
Sap. iii. 13, x. 1 (Pesh.).

69. *in iudicio uenientes*] Instead of *in iudicium
uen*. See Rönsch, p. 406. The MS. has *uenientis*
here, and *inspirationis* (pr. m.) v. 80; other instances
of this old spelling of the plur. are given above, p. 13.

uenisset, in the sense of *euenisset;* it is possible,
however, that the first three letters are merely echoed
from the previous clause, and that the true reading is *fuisset*, which satisfies the other versions.

70. *cum eo*] According to the Syr., Æth., and Arab.,
ex eo. Comp. *ex eo*, iii. 21, vi. 54, vii. 118 (48), A. and S.

71. *sensus* is omitted in the MS. after *crescit*,
and the corrector in perplexity has inserted *vel
sensum* after *intellege*.

72 Qui ergo commorantes sunt in terra, hinc cruciabuntur, quoniam sensum habentes
iniquitatem fecerunt, et mandata accipientes non seruauerunt ea, et legem consequuti
73 fraudauerunt eam quam acceperunt. Et quid habebunt dicere in iudicio, uel quo-
74 modo respondebunt in nouissimis temporibus? Quantum enim tempus ex quo
longanimitatem habuit Altissimus his qui inhabitant saeculum, et non propter eos,
75 sed propter ea quae prouidit tempora! Et respondi et dixi: si inueni gratiam
coram te, domine, demonstra, domine, seruo tuo, si post mortem uel nunc quando
reddimus unusquisque animam suam, si conseruati conseruabimur in requie, donec
76 ueniant tempora illa, in quibus incipies creaturam renouare, aut amodo cruciamur. Et
respondit ad me et dixit: ostendam tibi et hoc; tu autem noli commisceri cum eis
77 qui spreuerunt, neque connumeres te cum his qui cruciantur. Etenim est tibi thesaurus
operum repositus apud Altissimum, sed non tibi demonstrabitur usque in nouissimis
78 temporibus. Nam de morte sermo est: quando profectus fuerit terminus sententiae
ab Altissimo ut homo moriatur, recedente inspiratione de corpore ut dimittatur iterum
79 ad eum qui dedit adorare gloriam Altissimi primum. Et si quidem esset eorum qui
spreuerunt et non seruauerunt uiam Altissimi, et eorum qui contempserunt legem

75. demonstra, domine, *demonstra dne.* reddimus *reddemus* altered to *reddimus.*
in requie *ᶦⁿrequie* (final *e* over an eras.).
78. .est *ē* added above the line.
79. spreuerunt *inspirauerunt.*

72. *et legem consequuti fraudauerunt eam*] This reading is probably correct; comp. *nec enim uidetur uoluisse fraudare edictum*, Digest. 29, II. 42; *fraudandae legis gratia*, id. 35, I. 64; though the Syr. ـحمـܠ pointing to ἠθέτησαν rather suggests *frustrauerunt*. Comp. Ps. cxxxi. 11, LXX., Vulg., and Syro-Hex., and the use of *frustrari* in a similar context, Iren. IV. 9. 3, 12. 1 (ed. Stieren), Tert. *Apol.* v.

In the Arab. we must translate thus: 'have set up for themselves an opposite law,' and not with Ockley (and Hilgenf.), *have set up their pleasures as an opposite law;* for the word in question should be read لِذَاتِهِم and not لَذَّاتِهِم.

75. *...domine, demonstra, domine, seruo tuo*] The *domine* which is placed in direct antithesis to *seruo tuo* is struck out as superfluous in the MS.; yet it probably represents a Gk. word, for where the former *domine* stands, the orig. according to the Syr. would be δέσποτα κύριε, but there are signs of variations in the Gk. text, for these words have no equivalent in the Æth. and Arab., while the Lat. translator seems to have divided them between the two clauses. The formula is correctly rendered *dominator domine* in a similar context, chap. vi. 11, xii. 7, 8.

78. The Syr. supplies *hic* before sermo.
terminus] Comp. *terminum Dei*, x. 16, and Tert. *de pud.* XIII.
recedente inspir... dedit] Comp. Eccles. xii. 7.
adorare] According to the Syr., Æth., and Arab. *adorat*, which no doubt represents the original. The Lat. transl. may have read προσκυνεῖν for προσκυνεῖ.

79. *spreuerunt*] The MS. has *inspirauerunt*, which is unintelligible, and can only be a mechanical repetition from verse 78. Both the Syr. and Æth.

80 eius, et eorum qui oderunt eos qui timent eum, Haec inspirationes in habitationes non
81 ingredientur, sed uagantes erunt amodo in cruciamentis, dolentes semper et tristes.
82 Uia prima, quia spreuerunt legem Altissimi. Secunda uia, quoniam non possunt re-
83 uersionem bonam facere ut uiuant. Tertia uia, uident repositam mercedem his qui
84 testamentis Altissimi crediderunt. Quarta uia, considerabunt sibi in nouissimis repo-
85 situm cruciamentum. Quinta uia, uidentes aliorum habitaculum ab angelis conseruari
86 cum silentio magno. Sexta uia, uidentes quemadmodum de eis pertransient in cru-

80. haec *haec* altered to *hae*. inspirationes *inspirationis* altered to *-nes*.
84. considerabunt *considerabant* altered to *considerabunt*.
86. pertransient in *pertransientem* altered to *pertransiens*.

refer us to ἀθετεῖν, of which a common equivalent is *sperno*. I have therefore substituted *spreuerunt*.

80. *Haec inspirationes*] *Haec* is the original reading of the MS. both here and in chap. xiii. 40, as also of Cod. S. in chap. xii. 35, xiii. 25, 40. This form of the nom. pl. fem. occurs in Lev. xxvi. 45, Num. iii. 20, 21, 27, 33, iv. 31, xxvi. 7, 22, 25, 27, (hae∗) xxx. 17, xxxi. 16, xxxvi. 12, Cod. Ashburnh.; in Num. iii. 1, Cod. A. (= Amiat.) and S. (Vercellone, *Variae Lect. Vulg. Lat. Bibl. ed.*); in Jos. xix. 51, Cod. Amiat.; in Esth. x. 11, Cod. Pech. (Sabat.); in Job xviii. 21, Cod. Maj. Mon. (id.); and so *haec* should be explained in Ezek. xlvii. 12, *quoniam aquae eorum de sanctis haec procedunt*, Fragm. Weingart. (A. Vogel, *Beiträge zur Herstellung der alt. lat. Bibel-Uebers.* Wien, 1868). Comp. also Apul. *Metam.* iv. 2, Hildebrand's note, Lucr. vi. 456, Munro's note, and Ribbeck's Prolegom. crit. ad P. Verg. Mar. opp. maj., Index Gram.

The *recedente inspiratione* of ver. 78 smoothes the way to the use of *inspirationes* in the sense of disembodied souls. For the controversies which originated from identifying *inspiratio* with *anima*, comp. Diod. on Gen. ii. 7 : ὑπέλαβον ἔνιοι κακῶς, τὸ ἐμφύσημα τοῦ θεοῦ γεγενῆσθαι ψυχὴν τὴν ἀθάνατον, κ.τ.λ. (Catena in octat. et libr. Reg. Lips. 1772), and Philastrius *de haeres.* chap. 98 : *Alia est haeresis, quae dicit inspirationem animam esse, non inspirationem* (v.l. *-ne*) *in animam datam fuisse* .. Further references may be found in the note of Fabricius on the passage last quoted.

sed uagantes erunt] Since the Arab. as rendered by Ockley, *bound up with* (Hilgenf. *ligabitur cum*),

has been used by Volkmar to construct a highly improbable theory with regard to the verb in the original, it may be noticed that this version has simply ܡܥ ܟܣܘܒܝܐ 'numbered (or, reckoned) with.' —Read with the MS. له العايدين for له العابدين in Arab.[2]

tristes] We miss *per septem uias* after this word. Comp. verse 91. It is represented in all the other versions.

83. *testamentis Altissimi*] The words ܟܕܘܬܐ ܕܡܪܝܡܐ (comp. chap. iii. 32, v. 29) are absent from the Syr. Corresponding words are found in the Æth. and Arab.

84. The Syr. alone makes an addition at the end of this verse, which is thus rendered by Ceriani : *in quo corripientur animae impiorum; quia cum haberent tempus operationis, non subiecerunt se praeceptis Altissimi.*

84, 85. Hippolytus (ἐκ τοῦ πρὸς Ἕλληνας λόγου τοῦ ἐπιγεγραμμένου κατὰ Πλάτωνος περὶ τῆς τοῦ παντὸς αἰτίας) has worked out these ideas in detail: οἱ ἔγγιον ὄντες τοῦ μὲν βρασμοῦ ἀδιαλείπτως ἐπακούουσι καὶ τοῦ τῆς θέρμης ἀτμοῦ οὐκ ἀμοιροῦσιν, αὐτῆς δὲ τῆς ἐγγίονος ὄψεως τὴν φοβερὰν καὶ ὑπερβαλλόντως ξανθὴν θέαν τοῦ πυρὸς ὁρῶντες καταπεπήγασι, τῇ προσδοκίᾳ τῆς μελλούσης κρίσεως ἤδη δυνάμει κολαζόμενοι, ἀλλὰ καὶ οὗτοι τὸν τῶν πατέρων χορὸν (var. lect. χῶρον) καὶ τοὺς δικαίους ὁρῶσι, καὶ ἐπ' αὐτῷ τούτῳ κολαζόμενοι. (Ed. de Lagarde, p. 69.)

86. *quemadmodum de eis pertransient in cruciamentum*] There is great diversity in the transla-

87 ciamentum. Septima uia est omnium quae supradictae sunt uiarum maior, quoniam detabescent in confusione et consumentur in honoribus† et marcescent in
timoribus, uidentes gloriam Altissimi coram quem uiuentes peccauerunt et coram

87. uia *cruciamtum uia.* in confusione *in confusionem.* consumentur *consumuntur* altered to *consumentur.*
honoribus *honoribus* altered to *horroribus.* coram quem *coram quem* altered to *coram quo.* uiuentes *uidentes.*

tions of this passage; in the Syr. (*quia uident, quod
amodo eis praeparatum est, cruciamentum*) it is
little more than a repetition of verse 84, but just as
the via Vᵗᵃ adds to the via IIIᵗⁱᵃ the part borne by
the angels, so we might expect in the via VIᵗᵃ a
corresponding addition to the via IVᵗᵃ, and this idea
is expressed by the use of the causative form of the
verb in the Æth. *quod cogunt* [sc. *Angeli*] *eos cir-
cumire et uidere, quod amodo eis continget, cruciamentum.* Now the main difference between the
Lat. and the Æth. may be accounted for by supposing them to have been derived from the Gk. ἀπ'
αὐτῶν διακομισθήσονται εἰς τὸν βασανισμόν, the verb
having been taken as mid. (comp. διακομισθείς, διελ-
θών, Hesych. and Suid.), in the one case, but more
correctly as pass., in the other; the same compound
is used by Plato in a similar context: τίσεις δὲ αὐτῶν
τὴν προσήκουσαν τιμωρίαν εἴτ' ἐνθάδε μένων εἴτε καὶ
ἐν Ἅδου διαπορευθεὶς εἴτε καὶ τούτων εἰς ἀγριώτερον ἔτι
διακομισθεὶς τόπον. *De Legibus*, lib. x. p. 905.

The twofold office thus assigned to the Angels in
ver. 85, 86 is set forth at length by Hippolytus in
the work quoted above (ed. de Lagarde pp. 68, 69):
Τοῦτο τὸ χωρίον (sc. Ἅδης) ὡς φρούριον ἀπενεμήθη
ψυχαῖς, ἐφ' ᾧ κατεστάθησαν ἄγγελοι φρουροί, πρὸς τὰς
ἑκάστων πράξεις διανέμοντες τὰς τῶν τόπων προσκαί-
ρους κολάσεις....μία γὰρ εἰς τοῦτο τὸ χωρίον κάθοδος,
οὗ τῇ πύλῃ ἐφεστῶτα ἀρχάγγελον ἅμα στρατιᾷ πεπι-
στεύκαμεν, ἣν πύλην διελθόντες οἱ καταγόμενοι ὑπὸ τῶν
ἐπὶ τὰς ψυχὰς τεταγμένων ἀγγέλων οὐ μιᾷ ὁδῷ πορεύον-
ται, ἀλλ' οἱ μὲν δίκαιοι εἰς δεξιὰ φωταγωγούμενοι καὶ
ὑπὸ τῶν ἐφεστώτων κατὰ τόπον ἀγγέλων ὑμνούμενοι,
ἄγονται εἰς χωρίον φωτεινόν,.. οἱ δὲ ἄδικοι εἰς ἀριστερὰ
ἕλκονται ὑπὸ ἀγγέλων κολαστῶν, οὐκέτι ἑκουσίως πο-
ρευόμενοι, ἀλλὰ μετὰ βίας ὡς δέσμιοι ἑλκόμενοι, οἷς οἱ
ἐφεστῶτες ἄγγελοι ἐπιγελῶντες διαπέμπονται, ἐπονει-
δίζοντες καὶ φοβερῷ ὄμματι ἐπαπειλοῦντες εἰς τὰ κατώ-
τερα ὠθοῦντες, οὓς ἀγομένους ἕλκουσιν οἱ ἐφεστῶτες

B.

ἕως πλησίον τῆς γεέννης (quoted in part by Hilgenf.).
—I have introduced into this verse but one simple
emendation, *pertransient in* for *pertransientem*, but
it is not unreasonable to suppose that instead of
quemadmodum there stood originally q̅n̅m̅ (=*quoniam*) *amodo*, inasmuch as an equivalent to *amodo*
(ἀπ' ἄρτι) is found, though in a slightly different position, both in the Æth. and Syr. versions.

pertransient] Numerous examples of this form
of the fut. in compounds of *eo* are collected by
Rönsch, pp. 292, 293; we meet with both *transibunt*
and *transient* in the same verse, Luke xxi. 33, Codd.
Amiat. Forojul. (Blanchini, *Evang. quadr.*), Rehd. (ed.
Haase), Lindisfarne and Rushworth Gospels, and
also Cod. cclxxxvi. Corp. Xᵗⁱ Coll. Cambr., according
to the correction, but the latter verb was in this
case orig. *transibunt;* in Cod. Vindob. (Paulus, *Me-
morabilien* 7ᵗᵉˢ Stück) the two forms occur in inverted
order. The following instances have been noticed in
4 Ezra (including the extraneous chapters), *transient
oues* Cod. S., xvi. 33; *transiet*, xvi. 78 (e corr.) Cod.
A.; *exiet*, xvi. 9; *exient*, xv. 29, 30; *interiet*, ii. 26
Cod. S.; *interient*, xv. 57, xvi. 23 Cod. S.; *interient*
(*disperient* Cod. A.), xvi. 18; *perient*, vii. 20 Cod A.,
ix. 15 Cod. A. (e corr.), xii. 20.

The Bodl. MS. of Arab.² has here الجارى, also
ثواب in v. 83, both agreeing with Steiner's conj.
For the former the Vat. MS. has الجاى.

87. *detabescent*] This rare compound occurs in
Lev. xxvi. 39, Cod. Ashburnh. One authority for
the perfect is introduced in the last ed. of Forcellini,
detabuerunt, Ruf. vert. Orig. Hom. 2 in Ps. xxxviii.
The editor (De-Vit) however, according to his prac-
tice in citing the other compounds of this root, refers
it to a non-existent pres. *detabeo.* For verbs com-
pounded with *de-* in vulgar Latin, see Rönsch, pp. 188,

9

88 quem incipient in novissimis temporibus iudicari.   Nam eorum qui uias seruaue-

87. coram quem *coram quo -uo* written over an eras.

205, and Wölfflin, *Bemerkungen über das Vulgär-latein*, Philologus Bd. 34, pp. 161, 162. With the orig. reading *detab. in confusionem* comp. *et consumerentur in confusionem*, Jer. xx. 18, Cod. Amiat. The corresponding verb in the Arab. ينسبلوا has been rendered *shall be overwhelmed*, Ockley (*superfundentur*, Fabr.), *superabuntur* in Hilgenf. But the word is evidently connected in meaning with the *detabescent* of the Lat. version. Comp. the cogn. root שָׁבַל, and שִׁבְלוּל Ps. lviii. 9. Castell (*Lex. Heptagl.*) gives ' سَبَل IV. manauit ... VII effusus, protensus fuit. BB.' (the reference is to Bar Bahlul sub voc. ܡܥܒ̈ܕܢܘܬܐ.

[الراس] وتنسبل على الكتفين Cod. Cantabr.).

Arab.[2] has here لأبهم يدانون فى البهتان *dieweil sie in der Schande gerichtet werden.* Steiner. For the second word I would read يذابون 'shall be made to pine away.' This slight alteration brings the above compendium into harmony with all the other versions.

in honoribus†] It is not easy to explain satisfactorily the origin of the MS. reading *honoribus* (pr. m.), *horroribus* (e corr.). The plur. of *horror* is not in the Vulg., but we find in the Old Lat. *horrorum* (Gk. φόβου), Job xxxiii. 16, Cod. Maj. Mon. (Sabat.). By the correction this clause is drawn into parallelism with the following, but both the Syr. and Æth. versions lead us to expect *in pudore*, synonymous with the preceding *in confusione*. Ambrose also in his reference to this passage has *et pudorem et confusionem.* So that the Gk. had most likely the words αἰσχύνη...ἐντροπή, which are found together in the LXX, Ps. xxxiv. 26, xliii. 16, lxviii. 20, cviii. 29, also Isai. lxi. 7, Theod.; the corresponding verbs occur more frequently in parallelism. The Armenian is thus rendered by Petermann: *qua macerantur et consumuntur pudore et ignominia et circumdatae sunt intellectu et timore.* It may be mentioned here that the order is different in the

Arm. version, the above VII *uiae* being placed after the VII *uiae animarum iustorum.*

coram quem...et coram quem] Our MS. has in the first case, *quem* pr. man., and in the second, *quo* with the last two letters written over an erasure. I conclude, therefore, that *quem* was the original reading in both places. In like manner, *coram nos* is written, but *nos* is altered to *nobis* iv. 14, Codd. A. and S. Comp. also vi. 36, ix. 28, Cod. S. Rönsch (p. 409) quotes only one example of 'coram' with the accus., viz. 1 Thess. iii. 9, Cod. Clarom. To this may be added, Lev. xxvi. 7, Num. viii. 22, xix. 3, xx. 27, xxv. 6, Cod. Ashburnh.; Acts iv. 10, viii. 32, xix. 9, Cod. Laud. (ed. Tisch.); Deut. iv. 8, 1 Reg. xii. 2, Old Lat. Speculum (Mai, *Nov. Patr. Bibl.* I. 2, pp. 60, 114); Jer. xv. 9, Par. Palimps. Wirceburg. (ed. Ranke); Acts vi. 8, Cod. Par. Lat. 6400 G. (Old Lat. palimp. fragments at Paris, A. A. Vansittart, *Journ. of Philol.* II. p. 244); 1 Kings xi. 19, Cod. Reg. Suec. 1462 (Blanchini, *Vind. Can.* CCCXLI.); Juvencus, Sel. Fragm. XXVI. (Pitra, *Spicil. Solesm.* vol. I. p. 248.)

For *uiuentes* the MS. has *uidentes* here, and again in verse 94: on the other hand, in *uidentes,* chap. i. 37, and *uidisti,* chap. ii. 48, the 'd' is the result of a correction, having been originally written as 'u'.

88. *Nam eorum qui ...* (89) *commoratae*] So also in the Syr. MS. the masc. pl. ܕܢܛܪܘ is followed by the fem. pl. ܕܐܬܛܝܒ. Possibly the first clause in the original was so constructed that the gender of the subject would not be immediately apparent, as, for instance, τῶν γὰρ τὰς τοῦ ὑψίστου ὁδοὺς φυλαξαμένων. But from the nature of the case, we find in the Lat. as in the other versions great fluctuation of gender pervading the succeeding verses, and I have not attempted to introduce uniformity.

uaso also occurs vi. 56 Cod. S. For examples of *uasus* and *uasum,* see Rönsch, p. 260 (the ref. to Lucr. VI. 233 should have been given on the authority of Marc. Capella, as *uasis,* not *uasi,* appears to be the reading of the MSS). Add *uasi,* Lev. xiii. 59 Cod.

89 runt Altissimi ordo est hic, quando incipient seruari a uaso corruptibili.   In eo
    tempore commoratae seruierunt cum labore Altissimo, et omni hora sustinuerunt
90 periculum, uti perfecte custodirent legislatoris legem.   Propter quod hic de his
91 sermo: Imprimis uident cum exultatione multa gloriam eius qui suscipit eas,
92 requiescent enim per septem ordines.   Ordo primus, quoniam cum labore multo
    certati· sunt, ut uincerent cum eis plasmatum cogitamentum malum, ut non eas
93 seducat a uita in mortem.   Secundus ordo, quoniam uident complicationem, in qua

88. incipient *incipiet* altered to *incipient*.   uaso *uaso* altered to *uase*.
89. sustinuerunt *sustenuerunt* altered to *sustinuerunt*.   uti *uti* altered to *ut*.
91. multa *multā*.
92, 93. in mortem.   Secundus... *Item secundus*...
93. complicationem *complecationem* altered to *complicationem*.   qua *quo*.

Ashburnh., Ecclus. xxxviii. 30 Cod. Amiat.; *uaso*, Lev. vi. 28, xi. 34, xiii. 49, 52, 53, 57, Num. xix. 17, xxxv. 18 Cod. Ashburnh., Lev. xi. 34 Palimps. Wirceb. (ed. Ranke), 1 Pet. iii. 5 Old Lat. Spec. (Mai, *Nov. Patr. Bibl.* I. 2, p. 80), 1 Pet. iii. 7 Old Lat. Spec., Codd. Amiat. Tolet. Fuld., but *uasu* ib. Cod. Harl. 1772 (Griesbach, *Symb. Crit.* I. p. 369); *in uasum fictile*, Num. v. 17 Cod. Ashburnh.

89. *In eo tempore commoratae*] According to the Syr.: *In illo enim tempore quo commoratae sunt in eo*. Similarly the Æth.

cum labore] So the Syr. and Æth. In the Arab. this gives place to the usual phrase *in timore* (om. *eius* in Hilgenf.).

91. I have altered *multā* to *multa* on the authority of the Syr. and Æth. versions.

ordines] The versions are equally divided with regard to this word. From the Lat., Æth., and Arab., we might infer that τάξεις was used for the series that follows, while the Syr., Arab.[2] and Arm. require the same word as that used in the former series, viz. ὁδοί. Comp. especially the three leading versions in verse 99, where the two series are mentioned together; the Syr. is consistent in obliterating the distinction between the words, the Æth., as well as the Lat., in maintaining it.

92. *certati sunt*] For the deponent verbs, 'certor,' 'concertor,' 'supercertor,' see Rönsch, pp. 302, 303. A few more instances may be added: *certantur*, Gen. xlix. 6, Ital. Fragm. ex Cod. Σ (Verc. *Var. Lect.* I. p. 183); *certari*, Judg. iii. 2, Cod. Amiat.; *certabatur*, 2 Sam. xix. 9, Cod. B. [=Tolet.] and also

Codd. D. F. U. (Verc. *Var. Lect.*); *concertatur*, Cypr. App. de Spect. 3 (ed. Hartel).

In the Arab. بطغيان is rightly rendered by Ockley, *through the deceitfulness of*, and Steiner's correction *impietate* is uncalled for; see the verb in verse 48 (Ew. 45); comp. also Job xix. 4, Transl. Ant. Arab. (ed. Com. de Baudissin), and especially Cast. *Lex.* s. v. For *ut eos deflecteret*, in the translation of the Arab., read *ut declinarent*.

In justification of my departure from the MS. reading, *a uita. Item secundus*, I may remark that a comparison of the other verses in this and the former series shews that *Item* is an intruder before the ordinal, while the consent of the Syr., Æth. and Arab. versions goes far to prove that it is corrupted from *ī mortem*, which is to be appended to the preceding sentence.

93. *quoniam uident*] Instead of يرون, the MS. of Arab.[2] has ليرون; comp. the beginning of the neighbouring verses.

et quae in eis manet punitio] We can scarcely doubt, if we regard the context together with the Syr. and Æth. versions, that the Gr. text would be more correctly represented by *et quae eis* (or *eas*) *manet punitio*; this, I believe, was the original form of the Latin, the preposition having crept in by the force of association. A like faulty reading meets us in the Old Lat. vers. of Job xx. 26, *Et omnes tenebrae in eo maneant*, Cod. Maj. Mon. (Sabat.), from the Gk. πᾶν δὲ σκότος αὐτῷ ὑπομείναι. Comp. also Ps. xxxii. 20, *Anima nostra patiens est*

94 uagantur impiorum animae, et quae in eis manet punitio. Tertius ordo, uidentes
testimonium quod testificatus est eis qui plasmauit eas, quoniam uiuentes serua-

94. quod quo͡d. uiuentes *uidentes*.

in Domino, Cod. Sangerm., where other MSS. omit
in (Sabat.), the Gk. being ἡ ψυχὴ ἡμῶν ὑπομένει τῷ
Κυρίῳ. The construction of 'manet' with the accus.
and also with the dat., being rare in biblical Latin,
would be especially liable to give way to a more
familiar use of the word. A few examples of each
may be quoted, not inappropriate to the matter in
hand: (*a*) for the accus., Acts xx. 23, Vulg.; Lactant.
Instit. Epit. cap. LVII., *et illos aeternam poenam
manere*...(see Bünemann's note). (*b*) for the dat.,
Acts xx. 23, Cod. Bezae, μενουσιν μοι, *manen mi* (sic),
and the following passages, both from the translation of Rufinus, *et illis sciunt in iudicio grauiora
manere supplicia,* Clem. Recogn. II. 13; *Immortales tibi crede manere in iudicio et honores et
poenas,* Sexti Sententiae, No. 14 (ed. Gildemeister).
Comp. also the note on verse 95.

94. *quoniam uiuentes seruauerunt quae per
fidem data est lex*] The original of this sentence,
owing to the varying shades of meaning in πίστις, has
received different interpretations, which may be con-
veniently arranged in two classes according to the
construction of the word in question:

(1) where it is connected with the '*giving* of
the law,' as in the Lat., and in the Syr. also, where
the two words have become blended in the verb
ܐܬܗܝܡܢܘ, '(the law) which was entrusted to
them,' or, 'with which they were entrusted.'

(2) where it is connected with 'the *keeping* of
the law,' as seems to be the case in the Arm., from
Petermann's transl.: *quod magna fide seruauit, quae
datae ei sunt, leges.* In the Arab. also it is mixed
up with this clause. To the same class we might
refer the Æth., as exhibited in Laurence's transl.:
*quod seruauerunt fideliter in uita sua legem, quae
iis data est.* But when literally rendered it will run
thus: *q. s. in u. s. legem quae in fide quae iis data
est.* If the former of the relative pronouns be
omitted as superfluous, this version would range with
class (2), if the latter, with class (1). Neither Dillmann nor Prætorius supplies variants, but on referring

to the MSS. of the Brit. Mus., I find that one only
(Or. 490) supports the double relative of the printed
text, while all the others (Add. 16,188, Or. 484,
Or. 489, Or. 492, Or. 502, Or. 503, Or. 504, Or. 506)
omit it in the second place, and thus give their
authority in favour of ranking this version with class
(1). We may pass over the Arab. compendium and
the paraphrase of Ambrose, for 'πίστις' disappears
in the brevity of the one, and in the diffuseness of
the other. It will, perhaps, satisfy all the requirements of the case, if we assume that the words ἐν
πίστει were so placed in the sentence, that they
could be joined grammatically, either with the sub-
ordinate, or with the principal verb, as in the two
classes just described. Although the Lat. and the
Syr. versions both belong to the former class, yet in
the one the words in question were taken to denote
the state of mind in which, or the means whereby,
the law was received, *per fidem,* while in the other
they seem to have been understood in the sense of
'in trust,' 'as a charge,'—'they kept the law which
was given them in trust;' comp. Rom. iii. 2; 1 Tim.
vi. 20; 2 Tim. i. 12, 14; Herm. Past. Mand. III. etc.
When construed with the principal verb the same
expression naturally took the sense of 'in good faith,'
'faithfully,' as in 2 Kings xxii. 7, כִּי בָאֱמוּנָה הֵם עֹשִׂים
=ὅτι ἐν πίστει αὐτοὶ ποιοῦσι, LXX. The whole
clause, constructed as we have supposed, receives a
remarkable illustration from a passage in the Shep-
herd of Hermas (Vis. I. 3), which seems to be a
reminiscence of the one before us, and which in like
manner has given rise to two different interpretations; it stands thus: καὶ πάντα ὁμαλὰ γίνεται τοῖς
ἐκλεκτοῖς αὐτοῦ, ἵνα ἀποδῷ αὐτοῖς τὴν ἐπαγγελίαν ἣν
ἐπηγγείλατο μετὰ πολλῆς δόξης καὶ χαρᾶς, ἐὰν τηρήσωσι τὰ νόμιμα τοῦ θεοῦ ἃ παρέλαβον ἐν
μεγάλῃ πίστει (ed. Hilgenf. 1866, p. 7, comp. add.
p. 175); in the Old Lat. transl.:...*si seruauerint legi-
tima dei, quae acceperunt in magna fide* (ed. Hilgenf. 1873). Translators and editors have generally
attached the last three words to the verb which immediately precedes, and so Zahn: *dass die Christen*

95 uerunt quae per fidem data est lex. Quartus ordo, intellegentes requiem quam
nunc in promptuariis congregati requiescent cum silentio multo ab angelis conser-
96 uati, †atque in nouissimis eorum manentem gloriam.† Quintus ordo, exultantes
quomodo corruptibile effugerint nunc, et futurum quomodo hereditatem posside-

---

95. quam *quem* altered to *qua*. atque *et quae* altered to *atque*.

96. corruptibile *corriptibili* altered to *corruptibile*. futurum *futurum* altered to *futuram*. possidebunt *posseder̄*.

---

sie [die Gesetze Gottes] *in grossem Glauben emp-
fangen haben* ('Der Hirt des Hermas untersucht,'
p. 176). He also refers in connexion with the subject to another passage from the same work: οὗτος
γάρ ἐστιν ὁ διδοὺς αὐτοῖς τὸν νόμον εἰς τὰς καρδίας τῶν
πιστευόντων, Simil. VIII. 3. (From this point of view
reference might also be made to the following quotation from Papias : οὐδὲ (ἔχαιρον) τοῖς τὰς ἀλλοτρίας
ἐντολὰς μνημονεύουσιν, ἀλλὰ τοῖς τὰς παρὰ τοῦ Κυρίου
τῇ πίστει δεδομένας καὶ ἀπ' αὐτῆς παραγινομένας (v. l.
-νοις) τῆς ἀληθείας. Eus. *Hist. Eccl.* III. 39.)

On the other hand the structure of the preceding
clause, and the presence of the strong epithet before
πίστει, might be urged in favour of connecting these
words with τηρήσωσι, and accordingly we find the
passage thus rendered by the latest English translator: *if they shall keep with firm faith the
laws of God which they have received* (The Shep-
herd of Hermas, transl. by C. H. Hoole, 1870).

lex] Attracted, like *punitio* in the preceding
verse, to the case of the relative. See Winer's Gr.
XXIV. 2 (ed. Moulton). Examples of this construction (occasionally altered by later scribes) are found
in iv. 23 (*populum* Codd. A., S., *populus* C. 3, 7, 8,
10, 11, H.), vi. 54, vii. 32 (*animae* Codd. A., S., *animas*
C. 3, 5, 7, 8, 10, 11, H.), xiii. 49 (where Cod. A. has
gentes pr. m., *gentium* e corr.). Comp. also the next
note.

95. †*atque in nouissimis eorum manentem
gloriam.*†] Want of familiarity with the particular
usage of 'manet' mentioned above (see note on v. 93)
seems here also to have introduced corruption into
the text of the Lat. It will be seen that *atque* was
in the first instance written as *et quae;* if we take
this as the clue to the original construction, we may
restore the passage thus: *et quae in nouissimis eas*

(or *eis*) *manet gloria*. This emendation will bring
the clause into harmony with the Syr. and Æth.,
and will better explain the epithet which Ambrose
uses in his paraphrase of this verse: *et futuram
sui gloriam praeuidere*. Comp. especially his language in Extr. C.: *Alias manet poena, alias gloria*.

.96. I have recurred to the original reading
futurum (=τὸ μέλλον), which is supported by the
Syr. and Æth. The correction to *futuram* was
made at a later time, to help the reader through a
construction which had become obsolete. Among
the early attempts to get a Latin equivalent for the
Greek compound κληρονομεῖν, one was, to resolve it
into the two words *haereditatem possidere*, followed
by an accusative ; e. g. *et semen eius haereditatem
possidebit terram*, Ps. xxiv. 13 Rom. Martianaei,
Corb. et Coislin. (Sabat.), *ipsi haereditatem possidebunt terram*, Ps. xxxvi. 9 MSS. Sangerm. Coislin.
et Corb. (id.), *haereditatem possideamus nobis sanc-
tuarium Dei*, Ps. lxxxii. 13 MS. Sangerm., Psalt.
Corb. et Mozar. (id.). Again in the Old Lat. Speculum : *ut benedictionem hereditatem possideatis*
1 Pet. iii. 9 (Mai, *Nov. Patr. Bibl.* I. 2, p. 16), but
when quoted again it stands thus: *ut ben. hereditate
poss.* (id. p. 24). Comp. also Jer. xlix. 1 and Ezek.
xxxiii. 25 in the Cod. Amiat. In all these instances
we find a second and an easier reading, *haereditate
poss.*, which, confirmed as it was by the weight of
Augustine's authority, succeeded ultimately in sup-
planting the other. In a short discussion on the
best way of rendering κληρονομεῖν, that father says:
*Melius ergo duobus uerbis insinuatur integer sen-
sus; siue dicatur, Haereditate possedi; siue dicatur,
Haereditate acquisiui: non haereditatem, sed haereditate*, Enarr. in Ps. cxviii. 111. There is one other
passage in the 4th book of Ezra, where this archaic

bunt, adhuc autem uidentes angustum et [labore] plenum, quoniam liberati sunt,
97 et spatiosum, [quod incipient] recipere fruniscentes et immortales. Sextus ordo,
quando eis ostendetur, quomodo incipiet uultus eorum fulgere sicut sol, et quomodo
98 incipient stellarum adsimilari lumini, amodo non corrupti. Septimus ordo, qui est
omnibus supradictis maior, quoniam exultabunt cùm fiducia et quoniam confide-

96. angustum *angustam* altered to *angustum*. et [labore] plenum *et plenum*. et spatiosum [quod inci-
pient] recipere *et spatiosum recipere*. fruniscentes *frui nescientes*.
97. ostendetur *ostenditur*. amodo *quomodo*.
98. fiducia *fiducia* altered to *-tia*. confidebunt *confidebunt* altered to *confident*.

expression originally stood, though now disguised
by successive corrections, viz. chap. vi. 59, *quare
non haereditatem possidemus cum saeculo?* (ed.
Fritzsche). Here the *poss. nostram saeculo* of Cod.
S. leads us halfway back to the true reading, *poss.
nostrum saeculum*, which is required by the versions, and preserved in Cod. A. alone. In the latter
part of this verse it will be found that the Lat. has
been much corrupted. I have attempted to emend
it by the aid of the Syr., the Æth., and the extract
(D) from Ambrose, where he again takes up the
fifth order, and professes to give a verbal quotation.
The sense would be still clearer if, as the Syr. suggests, *a quo* were substituted for *quoniam*.

fruniscentes] This rare word has been corrupted
in the MS. to *frui nescientes*, and replaced by the
simple form *fruentes* in Ambrose. Besides the examples given in Lexicons, the verb occurs in Tob. iii.
9, MS. Regin. Suec. (Rönsch, p. 236), and Commo-
dianus, Instr. xxxvii., Carm. Apol. 298 (Pitra, *Spic.
Solesm.* I. pp. 29, 540).

97. Comp. Dan. xii. 3. Matth. xiii. 43.

amodo] The *quomodo* of our MS. seems to have
been suggested by the preceding clauses. The Syr.
and Æth. are in favour of the change to *amodo*.
Comp. Ambrose also, who has *qui tamen fulgor
earum corruptelam iam sentire non possit.*

98. *cum fiducia*] The MS. of the Arab. has
here بعظم ذاله. The latter word has occasioned
some difficulties. Ockley says: *There is no such
Arabick word that I know of, as occurs here in the
MS.* He accordingly left a lacuna in the translation which was filled up by Fabricius thus: (*in mag-
nitudine*) BEATITATIS. Ewald remarks: ذاله *ver-
schrieben für* ذاله *d. i.* ذاله: *ich bemerke dies
nur Ockley's wegen.* Steiner follows with a new
conjecture: Für ذاله ist nicht (wie Ewald will)
ذاله, sondern ذاته zu lesen: dass sie sich freuen
werden über die Grösse seines (Gottes) Wesens...
There can be no doubt, however, that so far as the
correction to ذاله is concerned, Ewald is correct,
though by translating it *mit höchster Lust*, in his
'Wiederherstellung,' which is here based on the
Arab., he fails to bring out the special meaning of
the word. After all, the form ذاله is given in
Castell's Lex., referred to the root داله fut. o. It
occurs in Bar Bahlul as the explanation of the corresponding Syr. word in this passage, ܦܪܣܘܡܐ,
and it stands in the Arab. of the Polygl., where the
Gk. has παῤῥησία, throughout the Epistles of St.
Paul and St. John, except in Eph. vi. 19, Phil. i. 20,
and Col. ii. 15, where مجاهرة is used, which is the
constant equivalent in the Acts of the Apostles, as
علانية is in the Gospels.

confidebunt] So *ostendebitur* vi. 28 Codd. A. and
S. and *surgebit* xvi. 10 Cod. S.; for verbs of the
3rd conj. with fut. in *-ebo* see Rönsch, pp. 291, 521,
and J. N. Ott, *Neue Jahrbücher für Philol. u.
Pädag.* 1874, p. 838. Add, from the Cod. Ashburnh.,
canebunt Num. x. 5; from the Old Lat. Speculum,
cadebunt Is. xxxiv. 4 (Mai, *Nov. Patr. Bibl.* I. 2,
p. 36), Prov. xvi. 2 (id. p. 48), Matth. xxiv. 29 (id.
p. 37); *metuebit* Ecclus. xviii. 27 (id. p. 49); from
the Cod. Bobbiens., *resurgebit* Mark x. 34 (*Wiener*

bunt non confusi, et gaudebunt non reuerentes, festinant enim uidere uultum
99 [eius], cui seruiunt uiuentes et a quo incipiunt gloriosi mercedem recipere.   Hic
ordo animarum iustorum, ut amodo adnuntiatur, praedictae uiae cruciatus, quas
100 patientur amodo qui neglexerint.   Et respondi et dixi: ergo dabitur tempus
animabus postquam separatae fuerint de corporibus, ut uideant de quo mihi
101 dixisti?   Et dixit: septem diebus erit libertas earum, ut uideant qui praedicti
102 sunt sermones, et postea congregabuntur in habitaculis suis.   Et respondi et dixi:

98.   reuerentes *reuertentes*.   uultum [eius] *uultum*.

99.   adnuntiatur, praedictae...*anuntientur praedictae*...   quas *quas* altered to *quos*.   patientur *patiuntur*.

100.   separatae *separati* altered to *separatae*.

101.   qui praedicti *quae praedictae* altered to *qui praedicti*.

Jahrbücher der Lit. Vol. 121), *exsurgebit* Mark xiii.
12 (id.); from the Cod. Amiat., *canebit* Hos. ii. 15.
The frequent use of this form is a marked feature in
the verses translated from the Gk. which are inter-
spersed throughout the Vulg. of Isaiah publ. by Jos.
Cozza (*Sacr. Bibl. Vetustiss. Fragm. ex Palimps.
Codd. Bibl. Cryptoferratensis*, Romae, 1867); e.g.
apponebitis xvi. 8, *ascendebit* xxxiv. 10, *bibebunt*
xix. 5, *cadebit* xxii. 25, *claudebit* xxix. 10, *confidebunt*
xvii. 8, *currebunt* xl. 31, *deponebit* xxxiii. 23, *de-
scendebis* xiv. 15, *dicebitis* xix. 11, *ponebit* xxii. 18,
supponebit xix. 16.

non reuerentes] The parallelism requires us to
read thus, by the omission of a single letter; similarly in Ecclus. xli. 19, Cod. S. Theod. has *reuerti-
mini* for *reuereamini*. Compare the phrase *con-
fundantur et reuereantur*, Ps. xxxiv. 4 (and verse
26 in Jerome, from the Hebr.), xxxix. 15, lxix. 3, in
which places αἰσχυνθείησαν (καταισχ—Ps. xxxix. 15),
καὶ ἐντραπείησαν stands in the LXX., similarly Ps.
lxx. 24. This emendation is also supported by the
paraphrase of Ambrose, *et sine trepidatione laetentur*. Referring to the other versions we find that
the above clause is either absent or obscured.

uultum [eius] The pronoun has been inserted from
the paraphrase of Ambrose supported by the Syr.,
the Æth., and Arab., as the following clauses would
be harsh without it.

gloriosi] A rendering of δεδοξασμένος by its ad-
jectival ἔνδοξος (e.g. 1 Pet. i. 8), instead of its strict
participial sense (comp. נִכְבָּד). The use of *gloriosi*

here may be illustrated by cases where it inter-
changes with a passive form, as *quam gloriosus fuit*,
2 Sam. vi. 20, whilst the same passage as quoted by
Ambrose in Ps. cxviii. stands thus: *quid utique
honorificatus est* (Τί δεδόξασται, LXX.), so also *glo-
riosior apparebo*, 2 Sam. vi. 22, *glorificabor*, in
Ambr. (ib.). Again, *nomen meum gloriosum est*,
Hieron. in Mal. i. 11, *glorificatum est* in the quotation of the same verse by Hieron. in Is. lix, Tert.
adv. Marc. III. 22, IV. 1, Aug. *Epist.* 93, 185 (see
Sabat.). Comp. also 1 Macc. ii. 64.

99.   The text of our MS. is here corrupt. I
have made a few slight changes, but something more
is necessary in order to disentangle the two clauses.
If we refer to the other versions, both the Æth. and
the Arab. suggest the insertion of *et haec* before
praedictae, a correction which might be proposed
with confidence if it were favoured by the Syr. also,
but this version would lead us to reconstruct the
Lat. thus: *et praedictas uias cruciatus patientur
amodo*... If we look merely at the Lat. text, the
addition of *sunt* might be accepted as a solution of
the difficulty, e.g., *praedictae sunt uiae cruc. quas*,
etc.   For *neglexerint* see note on *diligentia*, verse
37.   At the end of this verse the Syr. repeats, with
a few verbal variations, our eightieth verse (= end
of verse 39 Syr.). In the Arm. vv. 79—87 are transferred to this place (after *iustorum*).

100.   *tempus*] The Syr. alone has an unnecessary addition, *locus aut tempus*.

si inueni gratiam ante oculos tuos, demonstra mihi adhuc seruo tuo, si in die
103 iudicii iusti impios excusare poterint uel deprecari pro eis Altissimum, Si patres
pro filiis, uel filii pro parentibus, si fratres pro fratribus, si adfines pro proximis,
104 si fidentes pro carissimis. [Et respondit ad me et dixit: quoniam inuenisti gratiam ante oculos meos, et hoc demonstrabo tibi: dies iudicii dies decretorius est,
et omnibus signaculum ueritatis ostendet; quemadmodum enim nunc non mittit
pater filium, uel filius patrem, uel dominus seruum], uel fidus carissimum, ut pro

---

102. poterint *poterint* altered to *poterunt*.   uel *et* altered to *uel*.
104. [Et respondet—seruum] is not in the MS.   uel fidus carissimum *uel* written over an eras., *dus*
carisimum altered to *pro fido carissimus*.

---

102. *impios excusare*] In the Syr. ܡܪܚܡܐ
ܐܘܪ ܐܝܬܘܗܝ on which Le Hir remarks:
"*Interrogare impios.*" Gr. ἐρωτᾶν περὶ uel ὑπέρ, *bis
translatus est in Syr., prius falso per "interrogare,"
deinde rectius uoce* ܒܥܐ, *petere*. The Syr.,
however, does not deviate from the Lat., for the
verb must be taken as Aphel and rendered *excusare*. We have an instance of this rare use of the
form in Luke xiv. 18, 19, Cur. Syr. ܐܝܪܐܟܠܝ
'= ἔχε με παρῃτημένον *habe me excusatum*.
poterint = poterunt, so also vii. 14 Cod. D.
See Rönsch, pp. 294, 521. Add Luke xiii. 24 Cod.
Rehdig., Luke xxi. 15 Cod. Bezae (ed. Scrivener),
Cod. Amiat., Lindisfarne Gospels (ed. Skeat), *As-
sumpt. Mos.* IV. 8 (ed. Fritzsche). Comp. *erint* xvi.
66, 70, 72 Cod. S., Lev. viii. 32, etc., Num. iii. 45, iv.
7, 31, v. 9, etc. Cod. Ashburnh.

103. *fidentes*] This word corresponds to *fidus* in
the next verse, similarly *fidentibus* is opposed to
perfidis in *datur uelocius tutela fidentibus, perfidis
poena*, Cypr. *de Mortal.* xv. We have instances of
participial forms used as substantives in *discens =
discipulus* μαθητής, e.g. in Acts vi. 5 Cod. Par. 6400
(*Journ. of Philol.* II. p. 243), *audiens = auditor* ἀκροα-
τής, Jac. i. 25 Cod. Corb. (Sabat.). For other reff.
see Rönsch, *It. u. Vulg.* p. 107, *D. N. T. Tertullian's*,
p. 628, and Hartel's *Ind. to Cypr.* sub *Participia*.
The word *fidentes* seems to be merely a peculiarity
of the Lat.; there is nothing in the Oriental verss.
suggestive of any other reading than φίλοι. Comp.
for the argument, Hippolytus in the work before

quoted: τούτους...οὐ παράκλησις συγγενῶν μεσιτευ-
σάντων ὀνήσει (ed. de Lagarde, p. 71), and for the
language, *Constit. Apost.* II. 14: Εἰ δὲ πατέρες ὑπὲρ
τέκνων οὐ τιμωροῦνται, οὔτε υἱοὶ ὑπὲρ πατέρων, δῆλον
ὡς οὔτε γυναῖκες ὑπὲρ ἀνδρῶν, οὔτε οἰκέται ὑπὲρ δε-
σποτῶν, οὔτε συγγενεῖς ὑπὲρ συγγενῶν, οὔτε φίλοι ὑπὲρ
φίλων, οὔτε δίκαιοι [var. lect. δίκαιος] ὑπὲρ ἀδίκων·
ἀλλ' ἕκαστος ὑπὲρ τοῦ οἰκείου ἔργου τὸν λόγον ἀπαιτη-
θήσεται. Οὔτε γὰρ Νῶε... Hilgenf. quotes an illustration from Apocal. Esdrae, p. 27, ed. Tischend.

104. *Et respondit—uel dominus seruum*] This
passage is omitted in our MS., and the construction
of the following words has been adapted to the context by a corrector. The lacuna is here filled up
by the aid of the other translations.

signaculum ueritatis] ܚܬܡܐ ܕܫܪܪܐ
= σφραγὶς τῆς ἀληθείας, and in accordance with this
the Arab. كمثل الختم المحقق 'like the seal that
confirms the truth.' I therefore see no reason for
accepting the conjecture الحكم *gemäss dem die
Wahrheit entscheidenden Beschluss*, which is proposed by Steiner (Hilgenf. *Zeitschr.* XI. p. 429), and
embodied in the translation given by Hilgenf.

intellegat] According to the Syr. and Æth., the
original would be ἵνα νοσῇ, for which there seems to
have been a various reading, ἵνα νοῇ, which is represented in the clearest way by the Lat. and Arab.[2]
Examples of a similar confusion are not uncommon,
e.g. Chrysos. Hom. in Matth. 692 A, νοσήματα μανικά
(ed. Bened.), where Field restores νοήματα, and Seve-

105 eo intellegat, aut dormiat, aut manducet, aut curetur; Sic nunquam nemo pro ali-
    quo rogabit, omnes enim portabunt unusquisque tunc iniustitias suas aut iustitias.
106 (36) Et respondi et dixi: et quomodo inuenimus modo, quoniam rogauit primus
    Abraham propter Sodomitas, et Moyses...

104. curetur *curæ**.
105. Sic *Et diꝫ* added later before *sic.* rogabit *rogauit* altered to *rogabit.*

rus, hom. CIII. (Mai, *Scriptorum vet. nova coll.* IX.
731) Τὸν ταῖς κεφαλαῖς πολύν, τὸν πρῶτον νοήσαντα
τὸ ποικίλον τῆς πονηρίας καὶ πατέρα πάσης σχολιότητος
[leg. σκολ-], where Jacob of Edessa must have read
νοσήσαντα, as appears from his translation:

ܗܘ ܫܡܠܐ ܒܪܝܫ : ܗܘ ܩܕܡܝܐ
ܐܬܪܥܝ ܦܟܝܠܘܬܐ ܕܒܝܫܘܬܐ : ܘܐܒܐ
ܕܣܟܠܘܬܐ. (Add. MS. 12159 fol. 231. a. 2.
Brit. Mus.). Comp. also Cobet, *Novae Lectiones,*
pp. 283, 284.

105. *omnes enim portabunt...*] The Arab. has
بل كل احد يقوم بجملة, which is translated by
Ockley: *But every one shall stand for all (that he
hath done).* Steiner would alter the last word to
بعمله *sondern jeder Einzelne steht ein für sein
Thun.* I prefer to read بحمله 'each shall stand
with his burden;' this would involve less change,
and at the same time preserve an idea which is
expressed in the oldest versions.

EXTRACTS FROM AMBROSE AND JEROME.

(A) Comp. 4 Ezra VII. 36—42.

IBIMUS eo ubi paradisus est iucunditatis[1],......ubi nullae nubes, nulla tonitrua, nullae coruscationes[2], nulla ventorum procella, neque tenebrae, neque uesper, neque aestas, neque hyems uices uariabunt[3] temporum. Non frigus, non grando, non pluuiae, non solis istius erit usus, aut lunae, neque stellarum globi: sed sola Dei fulgebit claritas. Dominus enim erit lux omnium....*Ambr. de bono Mortis* XII. (*Ed. Bened.* I. *col.* 411).

   [1] *par. iocund. est.* GMPQ.   [2] *nulle choruscationes sunt* P.   [3] *narrabunt* Q.

(B) Comp. 4 Ezra III. 5; VII. 78.

Ambrosius Horontiano salutem....De quo tibi Esdrae librum legendum suadeo, qui et illas philosophorum nugas despexerit; et abditiore prudentia, quam collegerat ex revelatione, perstrinxerit eas (animas) substantiae esse superioris. *Ambr. Ep.* XXXIV. (*Ed. Bened.* II. *col.* 922).

(C) Comp. 4 Ezra VII. 80—87.

Ergo dum exspectatur plenitudo temporis, exspectant animae remunerationem debitam. Alias manet poena, alias gloria: et tamen nec illae interim sine iniuria, nec istae sine fructu sunt. Nam et illae[1] uidentes[2] seruantibus legem Dei repositam esse mercedem gloriae, conseruari earum ab Angelis habitacula, sibi autem dissimulationis et contumaciae supplicia futura, et pudorem et confusionem; ut intuentes gloriam Altissimi, erubescant in eius conspectum uenire, cuius mandata temerauerint[3]. *Ambr. de bono Mortis* X. (*Ed. Bened.* I. *col.* 408).

   [1] *Nam ille* Q.   [2] *uidentes* altered to *uident* E.   [3] *temerauerunt* GMPQ.

(D) Comp. 4 Ezra VII. 91—101.

Iustarum autem[1] animarum per ordines quosdam digesta erit laetitia[2]. Primum, quod uicerint carnem, nec illecebris eius inflexae[3] sint. Deinde, quod pro pretio sedulitatis et innocentiae suae, securitate potiantur, nec quibusdam sicut impiorum animae erroribus[4] et perturbationibus implicentur, atque uitiorum suorum memoria torqueantur, et exagitentur[5] quibusdam curarum aestibus. Tertio[6], quod seruatae a se legis diuino[7] testimonio fulciantur[8], ut factorum suorum incertum supremo iudicio non uereantur euentum. Quarto[9], quia incipiunt intelligere[10] requiem suam, et futuram sui gloriam praeuidere, eaque se consolatione mulcentes, in habitaculis suis cum magna tranquillitate requiescent stipatae praesidiis Angelorum. Quintus autem ordo exsultationis uberrimae habet[11] suauitatem, quod ex hoc corruptibilis corporis carcere in lucem libertatemque peruenerint, et repromissam sibi possideant hereditatem.........Denique sexto ordine demonstrabitur iis[12], quod uultus earum[13] sicut sol incipiat[14] refulgere, et stellarum luminibus comparari ; qui tamen fulgor earum corruptelam iam sentire non possit. Septimus uero ordo is[15] erit, ut exsultent cum fiducia, et sine ulla cunctatione confidant, et sine trepidatione laetentur, festinantes uultum eius uidere, cui sedulae seruitutis obsequia detulerunt : de quo[16] innoxiae conscientiae[17] recordatione praesumant gloriosam mercedem laboris exigui, quam[18] incipientes recipere, cognouerunt indignas esse[19] huius temporis passiones, quibus remunerationis aeternae gloria tanta refertur[20]. Hic ordo, inquit, animarum, quae sunt iustorum, quas[21] etiam immortales non dubitauit dicere in quinto ordine ; eo quod spatium, inquit[22], incipiunt recipere fruentes et immortales[23]. Haec est, inquit, requies earum[24] per septem ordines, et futurae gloriae prima perfunctio, priusquam in suis habitationibus quietae congregationis munere perfruantur[25]. Unde ait Propheta ad Angelum : Ergo dabitur tempus animabus, postquam separatae fuerint de corporibus[26], ut uideant ea quomodo[27] dixisti [?] Et dixit Angelus : Septem dies erit libertas earum, ut uideant, in septem diebus, qui praedicti sunt ser-

---

[1] uero EGMPQ.   [2] digesta lęticia ÷ (÷ over eras.) E. om. erit GMPQ.   [3] inflexi altered to inflexae EM. inflexi PQ.   [4] terroribus Cod. Reg. (quoted in Bened. Ed.)   [5] exagitantur MQ.   [6] tertium MPQ. [7] diuinae legis test. G.   [8] fulciuntur EGMPQ.   [9] Quartum EMP. Quartum ē Q.   [10] intell. incip. G. [11] exul. habet uberrimae EGMPQ.   [12] his EGP. hiis Q.   [13] eorum EGMPQ.   [14] incipiet Laur. Volckm. Hilg. Fritzsche.   [15] ordo his erit EP. ordo hiis erit Q. hiis ordo erit G.   [16] de q̃ E.   [17] constantiae EMPQ. [18] quem MPQ.   [19] om. esse GP.   [20] gloria tanta refertur EMPQ. tanta gloria largitur et refertur G. gl. tan. referatur Laur. Volckm. Hilg. Fritzsche.   [21] quos EMPQ.   [22] om. inquit G.   [23] fruentes et immortales sunt. EGMP.   [24] animarum Fabr. Laur. Volckm. Hilg. Fritzsche.   [25] gloriae ; Prima quiete congregationis munere perfruantur. Perfunctio prius quam in suis habitationibus. Unde E.   [26] corpore G.   [27] de quo modo for ea quomodo EGMPQ.

mones, et postea congregabuntur in habitaculis suis. Haec ideo plenius de iustorum ordinibus expressa sunt, quam de passionibus impiorum ; quia melius est cognoscere quomodo innocentes saluentur, quam quomodo crucientur flagitiosi. *Ambr. de bono Mortis* XI. (*Ed. Bened.* I. *col.* 408, 409).

[E = MS. 1. 3. 21. Emmanuel Coll. Cambridge.   G = MS. 114. Gonville and Caius Coll. Cambridge. M = MS. 5. A. xv. Brit. Museum.   P = MS. 193. Pembroke Coll. Cambridge.   Q = MS. 203. Pembroke Coll. Cambridge.]

(E)   Comp. 4 Ezra VII. 102—

Dicis in libello tuo, quod dum uiuimus, mutuo pro nobis[1] orare possumus[2], postquam autem mortui fuerimus, nullius sit pro alio exaudienda oratio, praesertim cum Martyres ultionem sui sanguinis obsecrantes, impetrare non quiuerint[3]. . . .

Tu uigilans dormis, et dormiens scribis: et proponis[4] mihi librum apocryphum, qui sub nomine Esdrae a te, et similibus tuis[5] legitur : ubi scriptum est, quod post mortem nullus pro aliis audeat[6] deprecari : quem ego librum nunquam legi. Quid enim necesse est in manus[7] sumere, quod Ecclesia non recipit ? nisi forte Balsamum mihi, et Barbelum[8], et Thesaurum Manichaei, et ridiculum nomen Leusiborae proferas[9], et quia ad radices Pyrenaei habitas, uicinusque es Iberiae, Basilidis antiquissimi haeretici, et imperitae scientiae, incredibilia portenta prosequeris[10], et proponis[11] quod totius orbis auctoritate damnatur. *Hieron. contra Vigilantium.* (*Opp. ed. Vallarsius,* II. *col.* 392, 393).

¹ om. *pro nobis* ABCDU.   ² *possimus* BCDU.   ³ *impetr. nequiuerint* ABCDU.   ⁴ *propinas* Fabr. Laur. Volckm. Hilg. Fritzsche.   ⁵ *tui* V.   ⁶ *gaudeat* Fabr. Laur. Lücke Volckm. Hilg. Fritzsche.   ⁷ *in manu* EF.   ⁸ *barbelo* ABCDEFU.   *barbellū* V.   ⁹ om. *proferas* CEFU.   ¹⁰ *persequeris* ABCDUV. *perquires* EF.   ¹¹ *propones* EF.

[A = MS. 6 C. xi. Brit. Mus.   B = MS. 6. D. i. Brit. Mus.   C = MS. 6. D. ii. Brit. Mus.   D = MS. 6. D. iii. Brit. Mus.   E = Harl. 5003. Brit. Mus.   F = Burney 322. Brit. Mus.   U = Dd. ii. 7. Univ. Libr. Cambridge.   V = Dd. vii. 1. Univ. Libr. Cambridge.]

ADDENDA.

PAGE 1, note 3. The Vatican MS. of the Arabic vers. (= Cod. V.), written apparently in the 16th century, proves to be a copy of the Oxford MS., Bodl. 251 (= Cod. B.), which is dated Anno Martyrum 1051 (= A. D. 1335). The relationship of these two MSS. might have been suspected from comparing the lists of their contents, e. g. 1 Ezra (= 4 Esdr. III.—XIV.), Ezra, Neh., Tobit, appear in the same order in both, (comp. Mai, *Scrip. Vet. N.C.* IV. p. 3 with Nicoll, *Cat. Codd. MSS. Ox. Bibl. Bodl.* p. 13). But Dr. Guidi's collation furnishes conclusive evidence of the origin of Cod. V.: e.g. in VII. 94 (Ew. 75, p. 33, l. 11) the word بها is nearly obliterated in Cod. B., it is absent from Cod. V. In VII. 95 (Ew. 75, p. 33, l. 13) the word الساعة in Cod. B. has lost portions of its last two letters, and in its mutilated form resembles السكب, which is the reading of Cod. V. In VII. 96 (Ew. 75, p. 33, l. 17) there are some defects in the MS., where the word stands, which Ewald takes to be المشا, in Cod. V. it is written والمسلك, and from the traces that still remain, we may infer that this was the original reading of Cod. B. In VII. 97 (Ew. 75, p. 33, l. 18) some strokes have been rubbed out from the middle of مستنيرة in Cod. B., the word consequently appears as منيرة in Cod. V. There is a hole in Cod. B. at the end of VII. 100 (Ew. 77), so that the last word is imperfect, but the points below the line are rather in favour of the reading قيل, as Cod. V. gives it, than of تقول, as Ewald edits. The words اه منك يا ادم are written by a later hand in Cod. B, at the foot of the page, where the last word is اخطات VII. 118 (48, Ew. 90), they stand after the same word in the text of Cod. V. The latter MS. differs from the printed text in reading والعالم VII. 70 (Ew. 62), هدا الامر VII. 75 (Ew. 66) and فانت اذا VII. 76 (Ew. 67), but it has been found on inspection to represent in these cases also, with but slight deviations, the text of Cod. B. In one respect the copy varies from the original, viz. by the introduction of a greater number of errors in orthography and

grammar: it has, for instance, ت for ث nearly always, ت for ث, ح for خ, ص for ض,
ز for ذ, sometimes ق for ك, as in تدرقه مسلوقه VII. 42 (Ew. 39), v. 3. Again, ابتهل
for ابتهال VII. 42 (Ew. 40), ينالون for ينالون VII. 47 (Ew. 44), ينالوا for etc., VI. 1, اجابنى احبنى for
الاولى for الاوله, هذه for هدا etc., v. 44, الاشيا for الشيا VII. 92 (Ew. 75). But though exhibiting a debased form of the language, the Vatican copy will be of some service in
supplying what has been obliterated or lost in the MS. of the Bodleian.

Page 2, note 2. Possibly another version has in like manner been printed and
neglected; for the list of books contained in the Georgian Bible, fol. Moskau, 1743,
seems to include the 4th of Esdr., disguised by a different enumeration[1]. It would be
interesting to have some trustworthy information on this subject. The Georgian translation of the Old Test. is said to have been made in the sixth century, from the
Greek, and to have been subsequently corrected from the old Slavonic.

Page 2, note 4. The Vatican MS. of Arab.[2] is stated to belong to the 14th century. It differs in many respects from the Bodleian MS., but especially in exhibiting
an unabridged form of the text, so that it will prove an important contribution to the
criticism of this particular version. A few examples of its readings are given below.

Page 3, latter part of note 5. I may here notice a modern Hebrew translation of
4 Esdr. XIII., written in rabb. char. at the end of Cod. 272, in the Library of De-Rossi
at Parma. It is thus described in the Cat. *Excerptum ex lib.* IV. *Esdrae Cap. xiii. ex
Bibliis christianorum, seu latinis hebraice versum, membr. et chart. in* 4° *an.* 1487. MSS.
Codd. Hebr. Biblioth. I. B. de-Rossi, I. p. 155.

Dr. A. Neubauer has kindly forwarded to me the following specimen of this
translation:

טופס העתקת מספר רביעי מיוחס לעזרא הסופר הנמצא בביבליאה נוצרית בספר רביעי מעזרא פרק
י"ג וזה לשונו

(1) ויהי אחרי שבעת ימים חלמתי חלום לילה (2) והנה רוחות עולות מיס לסער המון גליו (3) וארחה
והנה התחזק איש עם נבואות השמים ומידי כנותו להבין חרדו כל הנראים תחתיו (4) ובכל מקום אשר יצא
קולו בערו כל השומעים כאשר תבער ארץ בהריחה אש (5) וארחה אח'כ' והנה רגשו גוים לאין מספר מארבע
רוחות השמים להלחם עם האיש העולה מן היס (6) וארחה והנה חקק לו הר גבוה ויעף עליו (7) ואני

---

[1] ... "13, 14) die beyden (Bücher) der Chronik,
15) Esras, 16) Nehemias, 17) das 2te und 18) das 3te
Buch Esras, 19) Tobias" ... (Eichhorn's *Allg. Bibl.* I.

A.D. 1787, p. 168). I have not been able to find a
copy of the edition of the Georgian Bible here referred to.

בקשתי לראות את המלך׳¹ או את המקום מאין נחקק ההר ולא יכולתי. ⁽⁸⁾ ואח׳כ׳ ראיתי והנה כל המתקבנים
אליו להלחם אתו יראים מאד ואמנם העיזו פניהם להלחם ⁽⁹⁾ והנה כאשר ראה רגשת ההמון הבא לא הריס
ידו . . . ⁽⁵³⁾ זה פתרון החלום אשר ראית ובאשר הראית לדעת ⁽⁵⁴⁾ כי עזבת מחשבותיך ושמת עשתונתיך
לבקש את תורתי. ⁽⁵⁵⁾ ונפשך הביעות לחכמה ושכלך קראת קראת היות קטן מהכיל ⁽⁵⁶⁾ ע״כ הראיתיך הנסתרות
אשר עם ש׳ לא אכחד אמנם בעוד שלשת ימים אדבר עוד אליך ואבאר גדולות ונוראות ⁽⁵⁷⁾ ואלך ואעבור
בשדה מפאר ומשבח מאד לשם עליון והנוראות אשר עשה ⁽⁵⁸⁾ יושב וון [leg. ודן] את כל העולם כולו.
עד כאן נעתק מהמקום הנ״ל

I have just received, through the kindness of the Abbate Pietro Perreau, a transcript of the entire chapter, but the sample which I have printed will, no doubt,
be thought sufficient. This Hebr. version of Chap. XIII. appears to have been made
from an early printed edition of the Latin Bible, in which the abbreviations were
not always understood by the translator, e.g. he probably found in verse 36 *ōndet*²
(= *ostendetur*), which he took for an active verb², and in verse 55 *mr̄em* (= *matrem*),
which he expanded into *minorem*, and paraphrased³.

Page 5, line 7. The date of Cod. S. is inserted in the initial letter O, at the
beginning of Ecclesiasticus, (see *Nouv. Traité de Diplomatique*, III. p. 128).

Page 6, line 10. 'non réglées' rather 'réglées a la pointe sèche', but the traces
of the ruling are scarcely visible in some sheets.

Page 8, note 1. My friend, the Rev. H. B. Swete, B.D., Fellow of Gonv. and
Cai. Coll. Camb., has, at my suggestion, undertaken an edition of the Comm. of Theod.
Mopsuest. on the shorter epistles of St Paul. From his collation of the two MSS., I
will insert in these Addenda a few further illustrations of peculiar forms and constructions.

Page 10, note 3. Add to the list of contractions found in Cod. S. *dieb;, diẍ, ei'*,
enī, fr̄s, n̄, mⁱ, ōma, sc̄lm, uob̄.

I have been able to glean a few readings from some of the MSS. mentioned
below (p. 82, seq.).

Page 19, note 1. *sequenti precedente* VI. 12, Codd. Arras, Cambrai.

Page 19, note 3. *et pauor* IV. 24, Codd. Arr., Cambrai.

¹ מלכות is again the rendering of *regio* in verse
45.

² The words *Syon autem ueniet, et ostendetur*
(*ōndet*²) *omnibus parata et edificata* are thus translated :

ולציון אמנם יבא ויורה לכל העתידות והבנויות.

³ The two contractions, here referred to, occur in
a Venice Bible of 1478.

Page 19, note 5. om. *oro* VI. 12, Cod. Dou., om. *oro ut,* Cod. Orl.

Page 20, note 1. *uoluptate* III. 8, Codd. Orl., Dou., *pro ualidis* VII. 112 (42), Dou.

Page 20, note 3. *recipe* II. 40, Cod. Dou.

Page 20, line 25. *factus est* III. 17, Cod. Arr.

Page 20, line 26. *facit* III. 31, Cod. Arr.

Page 21, line 7. *tue enim creature miserearis* VIII. 45, Cod. Dou.

Page 21, line 12. *hunc sermonem* X. 20, Cod. Cambrai, *hoc sermonem hunc,* Cod. Arr.

Page 21, note 2. om. *in ea* XI. 32, Cod. Dou.

Page 23, note 1. The following observations on the word 'Arzareth,' XIII. 45, made by an English writer of the 17th century, seem to be unknown. I print them that they may hold their proper place in a résumé of opinions on the subject.

"... True it is indeed that I find the City of Arsaratha, mentioned both in Berosus fragments (I. lib. 3 ?), and in Ptol. (Geogr. l. 5, c. 13, et in Tab. 3 Asiae), placed neere the issue of the river Araxes into the Caspian sea: and it was perhaps one of the Israelitish Colonies, planted in the confines of the Empire of Assyria: for it may well be that Arsaratha is but יער שאריה [leg. עיר שארית], or הר שארית, that is the City, or the hill of the remainder: or perhaps ארץ שארית (the last letter of the first word cut off in the Greeke pronounciation for sounds sake), the Land of the remainder: but the tale of eighteene monthes journey, will no more agree with this City, then the region of Arsareth doth, with Geography or History." (*Enquiries touching the diversity of Languages, and Religions, through the chiefe parts of the World* by Edw. Brerewood, lately professour of Astronomy in Gresham Colledge, 4to, London, 1635, pp. 107, 108.)

Page 24, note 3. I refer in this note to the well-known couplet from Hudibras:

"In mathematics he was greater
Than Tycho Brahe, or Erra Pater."

There seems to be no good reason for supposing with Dr Z. Grey[1], that Wm. Lilly (1602—1681) is alluded to in this anticlimax. At any rate the bare assertion of some modern annotators of Hudibras, that such is the case, has the effect of keeping completely out of view the popular astrological tract, which under the name of 'Erra Pater' was frequently reprinted at London in the 16th and 17th centuries. A copy in the

[1] The principal argument on which he relies is an expression found in the 'Memoirs of the years 49 and 50,' p. 75 (publ. in the 2nd Vol. of *The Post-humous Works* of Sam. Butler, 1715), "O the infallibility of Erra Pater Lilly!"

Brit. Mus. is entitled, "The Pronostycacion for ever of Erra Pater : *A Jewe borne in Jewery*" ... (Robt. Wyer) London, [circ. 1535]. The significant addition to the name, and above all the fact, that we find essentially the same matter ascribed to the Prophet Esdras, in old French (CLXXVIII. 11, St John's Coll. Oxford, see Coxe's *Catalogue*), in Latin (MS. Hh. VI. 11 (11), Univ. Libr. Cambridge), and in Greek (*Notices et Extraits des MSS. de la Bibl. du Roi*, XI. 2, p. 186, and Tischend., *Apocalypses Apocryphae*, p. xiv.)[1] lead to the conclusion that 'Erra' is a corruption from Ezra[2].

Page 25, note 4. C. Paucker gives examples of *districtio* 'synon. seueritas; male enim interpretantur Lexicographi.' *Zeitschr. f. d. österreichischen Gymnasien*, 1874, p. 99.

Page 26, note 4. *et antequam estuarent chamini in Syon* VI. 4, Cod. Arras, ...*chiminop Syon*, Cod. Dou.

Page 31, line 5. Should these coincidences in reading between Cod. A. and later MSS. prove in the end to be too marked and too numerous to be explained by the considerations which I have suggested, then we must assume, that, when Cod. S., in its mutilated form, was adopted as the basis of the text, some other MS., allied to Cod. A., was occasionally consulted in difficult readings. The fact that the lacuna was not filled up from this source will be best accounted for by the supposition that the passage was suppressed for dogmatic reasons.

Page 32, note 1. *mira* III. 8, Codd. Orl. Arr. Dou.

Page 32, note 3. *non in usum fuerit* IV. 29, Cod. Arr., *non euulsum fuerit*, Cod. Dou.

Page 40, line 8 from below. There is an early date in a record of bequest inserted on fol. 1 of Cod. C. 8 (one of the three MSS. containing the curious interpolation *et heretici* V. 8, see above, p. 23, note 1), which is not noticed by Dean Cowie in his Catalogue of the MSS. of St John's Coll. Cambridge. It runs thus : "Clausa testamenti Magistri Roberti de Pykering quondam decani Ecclesiae Beati Petri Eborum, qui legauit hunc librum prioratui de Gyseburn, et obiit die Jouis ultimo die mensis Decembris, Anno Dni millió CCC^{mo} XXXII^{do}. *Itm delego* (altered to *do lego*) prioratui de Gyseburn Bibliam meam meliorem, pro eo quod libri monasterii fuerunt combusti in combustione

---

[1] Compare especially in all these places the section which in the English begins thus : "In the yeare that Janyuere shall enter upon the Sondaye the wynter shal be colde, and moyst."

[2] The same kind of astrological literature sometimes appears under other distinguished names, as S. Dionysius, and Ven. Bede (comp. *Catal. de la Bibl. de Valenciennes*, par J. Mangeart, p. 684).

Ecclesiae sue[1], *ita quod faciant anniuersarium meum singulis annis in perpetuum in conuentu.*"

Page 41, line 5. Here follows a supplementary list of MSS. which contain 4 Esdr. I.—XVI., or any part thereof.

BIBLIOTHECA SUSSEXIANA.

Lat. MSS. No. 4.[2] Bibl. Lat. 8×5 inches. Ff. 513, Saec. XII.—XIII. ... 'there are the four books of Esdras, and the prayer of Manasseh at the end of 2 Chron.' (*Pettigrew's Cat.* I. 1. 1827, pp. LXX., LXXI).

THE BRITISH MUSEUM, LONDON.

Cott. MS., Claud. E. 1. fol. Saec. XIII. A vol. containing treatises by Augustine, Arnulf (Abb. Bonae-vallis), Anselm, and Pet. Comestor, and at the end, 4 Esdr. I. II. ('Lib. Esdre prophete[3], filii Sarei'), 3 Esdr. ('Et egit Josias')[4], 4 Esdr. III.—XVI. (*Communicated by Prof. W. Wright*).

THE MINSTER LIBRARY, YORK.

XVI. D. 13. Bibl. Lat. 4to. Saec. XIII. Presented to the Library in 1833. (*Communicated by the Rev. J. Raine*).

THE CATHEDRAL LIBRARY, HEREFORD.

P. VII. 1. Bibl. Lat. fol. maj. Saec. XIII.—XIV. At the end of the N. T., 2 Esdr. (= 4 Esdr. I. II. 'Liber Esdrae prophetae secundus'), 3 Esdr., 4 Esdr. (= 4 Esdr. III.—XIV.), 5 Esdr. (= 4 Esdr. XV. XVI.). (*Communicated by the Rev. Dr. Jebb*).

THE CATHEDRAL LIBRARY, SALISBURY.

No. 127. Bibl. Lat. 10¾×7 inches. Saec. XIII.—XIV. 3 Esdr. comes between 4 Esdr. I. II. and 4 Esdr. III.—XIV. (*Communicated by the Rev. H. W. Pullen*).

---

[1] From an entry in a MS. missal of Giseburne, it appears that this fire took place A.D. 1289. (*Catal. of the MSS. at Ashburnham Place.* Appendix, No. 44.) Comp. also Dugdale's *Monasticon Anglicanum*, last ed. Vol. VI. p. 265.

[2] This MS. appears also as No. 32 in one of Thorpe's Catalogues for 1844.

[3] The word *secundus*, I. 1, is absent from this and from the following MSS., A. C. 4, 5, 9, 10, 11, H., L. 1, 2, 4, 5, 6, O. 1, 2, Edinb., Orl., Reims, Dou. This is another point, in which many later MSS. coincide with Cod. A. and not with Cod. S.

[4] Of the two Latin versions of 3 Esdr., viz. the 'Versio Vulgata' (*Et fecit Josias Pascha—secundum testamentum Domini Dei Israel*), and the 'Versio altera' (*Et egit Josias Pascha—secundum dispositionem Domini Dei Israel*), the latter, which was first published by Sabatier, is by no means uncommon in MSS. I have observed it also in the following: C. 1, 3, 4, 7, 9, 10, 11, L. 1, 2, 3, 4, 5, 6, O. 2, 5, Chartres 157, Orléans 3, 6, Reims 2, and Douai 3. In Orléans 10, the commencement is *Celebrauit Josias Pascha*. No. CXX., Bibl. Senat. civ. Lips., dated A.D. 1273 (*Et elegit Josias Pascha*), seems, from the short specimen forwarded to me by Mr. C. R. Gregory, to present a mixed text.

THE UNIVERSITY LIBRARY, EDINBURGH.

AC. b. 14. Bibl. Lat. 4to. min. Saec. XIV. 3 Esdr. (= 4 Esdr. I. II. 'Liber Esdrae prophetae filii Sarai'), 4 Esdr. (= 3 Esdr. 'Et fecit Josias'), 5 Esdr. (= 4 Esdr. III—XIV. and XV. XVI.). (*Communicated by J. Small, M.A., and the Rev. Dr. W. L. Alexander*).

THE LIBRARY OF ALL SOULS' COLLEGE, OXFORD.

No. II. Bibl. Lat., 4to. Saec. XIV. ...1, 2 Paralip., 1 Esdr., 2 Esdr. (= Neh. and 4 Esdr. I. II.), 3 Esdr. ('Et feciat [sic] Josias'), 4 Esdr. (= 4 Esdr. III.—XIV.), 5 Esdr. (= 4 Esdr. XV. XVI.), Tob. (*Communicated by Prof. Jul. Zupitza*).

BIBLIOTHÈQUE PUBLIQUE D'ORLÉANS.

No. 6. Bibl. Lat., fol. maj. Said to date from A.D. 1179 (Cat. par A. Septier, 1820), I was not able however, on glancing through the pages, to verify this statement. ...1, 2 Paralip., 1 Esdr. (= Ezra and Neh.), 2 Esdr. (= 4 Esdr. I. II. 'Liber Esdrae prophetae filii Sarei'), 3 Esdr. ('Et egit Josias'), 4 Esdr. (= 4 Esdr. III—XIV.), 5 Esdr. (= 4 Esdr. XV. XVI.), Judith....

BIBLIOTHÈQUE COMMUNALE DE LA VILLE D'AMIENS.

No. 2. Bibl. Lat. 8vo. Saec. XIII. Abb. de St. Acheul.—'On y trouve tout l'Ancien et le Nouveau Testament, avec ... le 3ᵉ. et le 4ᵉ. livres d'Esdras.' (*Catalogue ... par J. Garnier. Amiens. 1843*).

BIBLIOTHÈQUE DE TOURS.

No. 15. Bibl. Lat. pars. 4to. Saec. XIII. Saint-Martin, 5, ...1, 2 Paralip., 'les quatre Livres d'Esdras,' Tob. I—III. 4. (*Catalogue...par A. Dorange. Tours, 1875*).

BIBLIOTHÈQUE DE TROYES.

No. 621. 1°. Pet. Comest. Hist. Scol. 2°. Libri Esdrae 2ᵘˢ, 3ᵘˢ, 4ᵘˢ, 5ᵘˢ. 3°. Lib. Thobiae. 4°. Com. in Exod. fol. Saec. XIII. 'Clairvaux .... 2°. Les Livres d'Esdras, II., III., IV., V., sont les Livres III. et IV. autrement partagés que dans les imprimés.' 2 Esdr. (= 3 Esdr.), 3 Esdr. (= 4 Esdr. I. II.), 4 Esdr. (= 4 Esdr. III.—XIV.), 5 Esdr. (= 4 Esdr. XV. XVI.). (*Cat. gén. des MSS. des Bibliothèques publiques des Départements*, II. 1855, p. 262).

BIBLIOTHÈQUE PUBLIQUE DE REIMS.

No. 2. Bibl. Lat. fol. Saec. XIII—XIV. ...1, 2 Paralip., 1 Esdr. (= Ezra and Neh.), 2 Esdr. (= 4 Esdr. I. II., 'Hic est liber Esdre prophete filii Sarei'), 3 Esdr. ('Et egit Josias'), 4 Esdr. (= 4 Esdr. III.—XIV.), 5 Esdr. (= 4 Esdr. XV. XVI.), Judith...

BIBLIOTHÈQUE DE LA VILLE D'ARRAS.

No. 785 (ol. 743). Bibl. Lat. 8vo. Saec. XIV. Mon. S. Vedast. ...1, 2 Paralip., Or. Man., 1 Esdr., 2 Esdr. (= Neh.), 3 Esdr. ('Et fecit Josias'), Apocri. (= 4 Esdr. I. II. 'Liber Esdrae prophetae secundus filii Sarei,' 4 Esdr. III—XIV. beginning with a capital letter, and 4 Esdr. XV. XVI. beginning with a capital), Judith...

BIBLIOTHÈQUE DE DOUAI.

No. 3[1]. Bibl. Lat. fol. min. Saec. XIV. ...1, 2 Paralip., Or. Man., 1 Esdr., Neh., 2 Esdr. (= 4 Esdr. I. II.), 3 Esdr. ('Et egit Josias'), 4 Esdr. (= 4 Esdr. III.—XIV.), 5 Esdr. (= 5 Esdr. XV. XVI.). Hester....

BIBLIOTHÈQUE DE CAMBRAI.

No. 270. Bibl. Lat. in 5 vols. fol. Saec. XIV.—XV. ...1, 2 Paralip., Or. Man., 1 Esdr., Neh., 2 Esdr. (= 3 Esdr. 'Et fecit Josias'), Esdre (= 4 Esdr. I.—XVI.). Tobias...

BIBLIOTHÈQUE DE VALENCIENNES.

No. 2. A. 3. 30, 31. Bibl. Lat., 2 vol., fol. Saec. XVI. St Amand. ...1, 2 Paralip., 1 Esdr., 2 Esdr., 3 Esdr., 4 Esdr., Tob..... 'Ces deux magnifiques volumes doivent tenir le premier rang parmi ceux que George d'Egmond, 71e Abbé de St Amand, fit confectionner durant sa prélature.' (Catalogue ... par J. Mangeart. Paris, 1860).

UNIVERSITÄTS-BIBLIOTHEK, ERLANGEN.

No. 610, 611. Bibl. Lat. 2 Bde. fol. Saec. XIV. ... 1, 2 Paralip., 1 Esdr., Neh., 2 Esdr. (= 4 Esdr. I. II. ?), 3 Esdr., 4 Esdr. ('vom vierten ist blos der Anfang des dritten Kapitels geschrieben') Tob..... (Handschriften-Katalog .... bearb. von J. C. Irmischer, Frankf. a/m. 1852).

UNIVERSITÄTS-BIBLIOTHEK, LEIPZIG.

No. 4. Bibl. Lat. fol. min. Saec. XV. ... 1, 2 Paralip., Or. Man., Esdr., Neh., Confessio Esdr., 3 Esdr., 2 Esdr. (= 4 Esdr. I.—XVI.)[2] Thob..... (Communicated by Mr. Caspar René Gregory).

[1] In the Catalogue of the MSS. of the Douai Library by H. R. Duthilloeul, 8vo., Douai, 1846, no mention is made of the presence of 4 Esdr. in this MS., but on the other hand No. 10, Bibl. Lat. pars, fol. Saec. X. is stated to contain ...'Paralip. (duo libri), Esdras (quatuor l.), Hester'.... As a MS. of this age would rank next in importance to Codd. A. and S., I made a point of examining it, while this sheet was passing through the press, and found that it never included more of Esdras than the two canonical books (Ezra and Neh.).

[2] From the omission of ego Salathiel qui et Esdras, III. 1, and the presence of cubiculo for cubili, ib., coupled with the fact that the whole is divided into XVI. Chapters, I conclude that this MS., like those mentioned above, p. 41, l. 1, merely represents the printed text of the Vulgate.

BIBLIOTHECA PALAT. VINDOBON.

Bibl. Lat., 8vo. min. Saec. XIV. 'Post L. Nch. fol. 247 reperiuntur duo Esdrae apocryphi, qui hic Secundus et Tertius inscribuntur.' (*Codd. MSS. Theologici .... Lat. ... rec ... M. Denis.* II. 1. No. XXIX. *Vindob.* 1799).

Bibl. Lat. fol. Saec. XV. 'Esdras in Libros V. dividitur.' 3 Esdr. (= 4 Esdr. I. II. and 3 Esdr.), 4 Esdr. (= 4 Esdr. III.—XIV.), 5 Esdr. (= 4 Esdr. XV. XVI.). (*Id.* I. 1. *No.* XVI. *Vindob.* 1793.)

Bibl. Lat., fol. Saec. XV. 'a quodam qui Joh. Hussi placita sectabatur, ut videtur, perscripta.' Esdr., Neh., 2 Esdr. (= 3 Esdr.), 3 Esdr. (= 4 Esdr. I. II.), 4 Esdr. (= 4 Esdr. III—XVI.). (*Id.* I. 1. No. XVIII.).

Bibl. Lat., 4to. Saec. XIV. '.... Paralip., subjecta in marg. Manassis Oratione, Esdras et Neh., Confessio Esdre desumta ex eius Libro IV. apocr. c. 8. a v. 20—37. non sine varietate ab editis. Tum Prov.'... (*Id.* II. 1. No. XVII.).

Bibl. Lat. pars I., fol. min. Saec. XV. 'Post Libr. Neh. Incipit confessio Esdre, quae nihil est aliud, quam Excerptum ex apocrypho eius Libro IV. c. 8. a v. 20. ad v. 37. rarissime in aliis Codicibus obuium, et dictione varians ab Editis[1] .... Hanc Confessionem excipit Lib. III. Esdrae hic dictus II.' (*Id.* II. 1. No. XLIII.).

D. MARCI BIBLIOTHECA, VENET.

Cod. V. Bibl. Lat., 4to. min. Saec. circ. XV. 'Esdrae Liber IV. mutilus est fine, et uariam exhibet ab editis lectionem.' (*Latina et Italica D. Marci Bibliotheca Codicum MSS.* 1741.)

At least 5 MSS. of 4 Esdr. were consulted for the Vulgate edited by the theologians of Louvain, Antwerpiae, 1573 etc. The scanty list of various readings selected is reprinted in Walton's Polyglot, vol. VI.

On one occasion MS. authority is expressly quoted on the margin of our Auth. Vers. (see marginal note to IV. 51).

The position which 4 Esdr. occupies in the MSS. may be here briefly noticed. It is generally found in company with the other books of Esdr. after Chron. (the prayer of Manasseh frequently intervening). In C. 5 the books of Esdr. come after Malachi,

---

[1] The text is of the same type as that of the MSS. mentioned above, p. 34. This may be seen from the specimen which is given :

Domine, qui habitas in eternum, cuius oculi elati et superiora in aere, cuius thronus inestima- *bilis et claritas incomprehensibilis, cui astant exercitus angelorum cum tremore, quorum seruacio in uento et in igne conuertetur, cuius uerbum firmum et dicta perseuerantia,* &c. 4 Esdr. VIII. 20—22.

and in L. 4, O. 1, after Esther. In C. 8, the 1st, 2nd (= Neh.), and 3rd of Esdras are in their usual place after Chron. and Or. Man.; while 2 Esdr. (= 4 Esdr. I. II.), 4 Esdr. (= 4 Esdr. III.—XIV.) and 5 Esdr. (= 4 Esdr. XV. XVI.), form an Appendix at the end of the New Test. On the other hand, in C. 9 the Canonical books of Ezra and Neh. have been omitted in their proper places, and are supplied in a different hand at the end of the Volume.

The order of sequence in the several books of Esdr., which Cod. S. presents, is as follows: (1, 2 Paralip.), 1 Ezra (= Ezra, Neh.), 3 Ezra III. IV. V. 1—3 (this extract is written in smaller characters, and fills one page only), 2 Ezra (= 4 Esdr. I. II.), 3 Ezra (= 3 Esdr. I. II. 1—15), 4 Ezra (= 4 Esdr. III.—XIV.), 5 Ezra (= 4 Esdr. XV. XVI.), (Hester).

The peculiar way in which chapters from the 3rd book are here distributed seems to be hinted at by the Benedictine editors of Ambrose, in the vague description which they give of a St. Germ. MS. which I have proposed to identify with Cod. S. (see above, p. 4, note 1). The ambiguity thus created with regard to the place in which this book should stand, was probably the origin of its varying position in later copies. In many cases 3 Esdr. comes after 2 Esdr. (= 4 Esdr. I. II.), and before 4 Esdr. (= 4 Esdr. III.—XIV.), as in Codd. C. 1, 4, 5, 7, 9, 10, 11, L. 1, 2, 5, 6, O. 1, 2, 5, also in the Cott., Hereford, Salisb., Edinb., All Souls, Orl., Reims, Douai and Vindob. (XVI.) MSS.

In other cases 3 Esdr. precedes 4 Esdr. I. II., (which is then followed immediately by 4 Esdr. III.—XIV.), as in C. 6, 12, D., L. 4, 7, O. 3, 6, 7, T., W., and in the Troyes, Arras, Cambrai, Leipzig and Vindob. (XVIII.) MSS. (3 Esdr. also comes before 4 Esdr. I. II. in C. 13, 14.) This is also the order of the books in Cod. A. (see above, p. 6)

It is interesting to notice that the MSS. (C. 6, 12, L. 7, O. 3, T., W., Arras and Cambrai), which were grouped together by internal evidence, have also this external distinction in common.

Page 42, H. A notice of this MS. may be found in an 'Account of the MS. Library at Holkham, by W. Roscoe' (*Transactions of the Royal Society of Literature*, Vol. II. (1834), p. 356).

Verse 37. In Arab². Cod. Vat. has تخوفوا for تجرعوا Cod. Bodl.
Verse 38. *in contra*, see Rönsch, pp. 235, 519. Comp. *in palam* XIV. 45.
Verse 38. In Arab². after الكبير ins. الذى هو القضا اليوم from Cod. Vat.

Verse 40, note 2. In a late Latin version of the 'Historia septem sapientum,' the style of which is thus characterized: "die ganze Schrift ist durch und durch romanisch, speciell italienisch, gedacht und nur die äussere Hülle lateinisch," we meet with the expressions *de sero* and *uno autem sero*. (Mussafia, *Beiträge zur Lit. der Sieben weisen Meister—Sitzungsberichte der Wiener Akad.* 1868, pp. 96 and 114).

Verse 41, note 3. The Vat. MS. has لناتس for لنائس, thus giving another proof of its dependance on the Bodleian MS., for the additional point in ق has been left from the ز which is erased in the latter MS.—It is just possible that Ockley in rendering this word by 'blast,' may have had in view a supposed form ليلفس (λαῖλαψ), which closely follows the ductus literarum.

Verse 41. The order is different in the Cod. Vat. of Arab[2]., which reads ولا مطر ولا برد ولا حر ولا ظل ولا زرع. (Both MSS. have ظل for طل).

Verse 42. In Arab[2]. Cod. Vat. has ويروا الناس for ويري الخلق Cod. Bodl.

Verse 47. Instances of confusion between μέλει and μέλλει are very common. See the various readings in Matth. XXII. 16, Mar. IV. 38, etc., Euseb. Eclogae Proph. III. 30 (p. 132, l. 13, ed. Gaisford), Chrysost. Hom. in Matth. 723 E., 833 D. (ed. Field). Comp. also Chrysost. Hom. in Epist. ad Rom. 583 C. (ed. Field), and Alb. Jahn's *Methodius Platonizans* (1865), p. 65.

Verse 66. *Multum enim melius.* Comp. also *quantumque minor*, Apul. de Magia Cap. LXIX. (note in Hildebrand's ed.), and *quantum et maior*, which is the reading of the Cod. Harl. in Theod. Mops. in Eph. I. 23. (*Spic. Sol.* I. 107, col. 2, l. 7).

Verse 69, note 1. This old plur. termination -*is* would naturally give rise to some confusion. I seem to see an instance of this in XIII. 4 *qui audiebant uoces eius*, where the original text was probably *uocis eius*, (the gen. after *audio* in imitation of the Greek, see Rönsch, p. 438)[1], which was mistaken for a plural. The oriental versions all have the subst. in the singular.

Verse 82. *reuersionem bonam facere.* The construction of this clause is peculiar to the Lat. The Syr. ('conuerti et bona facere') no doubt represents the orig. The error of the Latin translator might easily have arisen from mistaking ἐπιστρέφει ἢ ἀγαθοποιεῖν (or, ...ἀγαθὸν ποιεῖν) for ἐπιστροφὴν ἀγαθὴν ποιεῖν.

Verse 87. 'Septima uia est *omnium* quae supradictae sunt *uiarum maior*.' The construction is varied in verse 98, thus: 'Septimus ordo, qui est *omnibus supradictis*

---

[1] Similarly, *exaudiuit me Deus, ancillae* [-*le* S.] *tuae* IX. 45, Codd. A. (pr. m.), S., and *et intellege sermonum meorum* VIII. 19 Codd. A. (pr. m.), S. (Comp. σύνες τῆς κραυγῆς μου, Ps. V. 1.)

maior"[1]. In the other chapters also the comparative is followed either by the gen., as in Gk. (v. 13, vi. 31, xi. 4, 29, xii. 13, 45, xiv. 13), or by the abl. (viii. 30, so also ii. 43).

Verse 87, note 1. In the Arab. version Cod. V. has ينسلبوا instead of ينسبلوا. There are other examples of erroneous transposition of letters in this copy, as تركيس for تكريس vii. 108 (Ew. 83), and يطبلنى for يطلبنى xiv. 36.

Verse 89, note 1. *In eo tempore commoratae seruierunt....* As the clause at present stands, it is not unlikely that *commoratae* was taken by the scribe as equivalent to *commorationis*. I have not found elsewhere an instance of *commorata* used as an abstr. subst., like the analogous forms: *defensa, extensa, missa, remissa, puncta,* etc., see Rönsch, p. 83, and the remarks of J. N. Ott in *Neue Jahrbücher f. Philologie u. Pädag.* 1874, pp. 782, 783. In xiv. 13, Cod. S. has *corrupte,* where Cod. A. has *corruptio*^{ni} and the Text. Vulg. *corruptelae.*

Verse 89. *uti* (= *ut*). This older form occurs again, chap. xi. 46, also in Num. xxvii. 20, Cod. Ashburnh., and in the Vulg. of Philem. 14.

Verse 93. *complicationem.* Only two authorities have hitherto been cited for the use of this substant. viz. Cael. Aurelian. 4 Chron. 26, and Augustin. 1. Music. n. 19.

Verse 93, note 2. The original reading of Cod. A. in iii. 22, *mansit in malignum* is another illustration of this tendency to insert *in* after *maneo.* To the examples under (a) may be added: *Si quidem et* [Codd. Amb. Harl.] *illos, si solummodo non obedierunt fidei, poena maneat, quanto magis illos qui....* Theod. Mopsuest. in 1 Thess. v. 8.

Verse 96, note 1. The Latin and Anglo-Saxon Psalter of the Univ. Library, Cambridge, Saec. xi. (Ff. i. 23), as well as the Rom. version in the Canterbury Psalter of Trin. Coll. Cambridge, Saec. xii. (R. 17. 1), have likewise *haereditatem* altered to *haereditate* in Ps. xxiv. 13. The latter has also *hereditatem* in Ps. lxxxii. 13. The Psalt. Veron. has *haereditatem possidebunt terram* in Ps. xxxvi. 22 (Blanchini, *Vind. Canon.*).

Verse 102, note 2. The form *poterint* occurs in both the MSS. of the Lat. transl. of Theod. Mopsuest. on the shorter Epistles of St. Paul; in the Amiens MS., *pot$\overset{i}{u}$erunt* 1 Tim. v. 10, and *pot$\overset{i}{e}$runt* 1 Tim. v. 24 (Comp. *er$\overset{v}{i}$nt* 1 Tim. v. 15), in the Harl. MS., Gal. i. 1, and *pot$\overset{i}{u}$erint* 2 Thess. ii. 6.

---

[1] The two constructions stand in juxta-position in the Lat. of Cod. Bezae, Luke vii. 28, John xiii. 16, Matth. xii. 41, 42. (Comp. *Cod. Bezae, ed. Scrivener,* p. xxxix.)

INDEX I.

(In all cases the Pages of this work are referred to; n. indicates a foot-note).

12

INDEX II.

GREEK.

SYRIAC.

ARABIC.

دالة, 70 n.

ذاب (iv.), 66 n.

سبل (vii.), 66 n.

طغيان, 67 n.

لنافس, 57 n., 87

نياح, 55 n.

INDEX III.

CORRIGENDA.

Page 3, col. 2, line 24 from below. For *In patris* (ed. Bas.), the Bologna ed. (1496) has correctly *In primis*.

Page 13, line 16. For IV. 23 read IV. 23*.

—— note 2. Dele *cogitationis* XVI. 55.

Page 14, line 17. For XVI. 48 read XVI. 48*.

Page 15, line 19. For *quessiui* read *quaessiui*.

Page 18, line 19. For *cum eo* read *cum ea*.

Page 36, lines 2 & 4. Cod. S. has *relinquentur*.

—— line 2. For *et singulis* read *in singulis*.

—— lines 2 & 3. For *quatuor* read *quattuor*.

Page 40, line 14. Transfer *&* from line 15 to the end of line 14.

—— line 15. Dele *?* at the end of the line.

Page 41, line 25. For *Ignace* read *Ignazio*.

Page 42, col. 2, line 11 from below. For A. I. 12 read A. I. 14.

Page 67, line 4. For *Imprimis* read *Inprimis*.

Page 82, note 3. For *Edinb.* read *York, Edinb.*

For EU product safety concerns, contact us at Calle de José Abascal, 56–1°, 28003 Madrid, Spain or eugpsr@cambridge.org.